Atlantic City

Atlantic City

by

Dirk Vanderwilt

Atlantic City, 4th Edition (*Tourist Town Guides*®)
© 2010 by Dirk Vanderwilt

Published by:
Channel Lake, Inc., P.O. Box 1771, New York, NY 10156-1771
http://www.channellake.com

Author: Dirk Vanderwilt
Editorial and Page Layout: Quadrum Solutions (http://www.quadrumltd.com)
Cover Design: Julianna Lee
Front Cover Photos:
"The Show at The Pier Shops" © Dirk Vanderwilt
"Walkway to the Beach" © iStockphoto.com/loraseverson
"Absecon Lighthouse" © Dirk Vanderwilt
Back Cover Photo:
"Boardwalk Hall" © Dirk Vanderwilt

Published in April, 2010

ISBN-13: 978-1-935455-00-4

Disclaimer: The information in this book has been checked for accuracy.
However, neither the publisher nor the author may be held liable for errors
or omissions. *Use this book at your own risk.* To obtain the latest information, we
recommend that you contact the vendors directly. If you do find an error, let
us know at corrections@channellake.com

Channel Lake, Inc. is not affiliated with the vendors mentioned in this book,
and the vendors have not authorized, approved or endorsed the information
contained herein. This book contains the opinions of the author, and your
experience may vary.

For more information, visit http://www.touristtown.com

Help Our Environment!

Even when on vacation, your responsibility to protect the environment does not end. Here are some ways you can help our planet without spoiling your fun:

★ Ask your hotel staff not to clean your towels and bed linens each day. This reduces water waste and detergent pollution.

★ Turn off the lights, heater, and/or air conditioner when you leave your hotel room.

★ Use public transportation when available. Tourist trolleys are very popular, and they are usually cheaper and easier than a car.

★ Recycle everything you can, and properly dispose of rubbish in labeled receptacles.

Tourist towns consume a lot of energy. Have fun, but don't be wasteful. Please do your part to ensure that these attractions are around for future generations to visit and enjoy.

The Atlantic City Boardwalk is the country's first boardwalk.

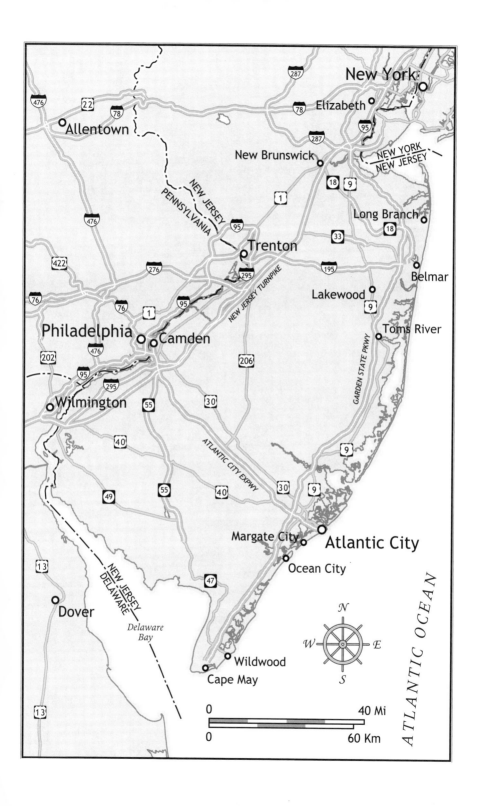

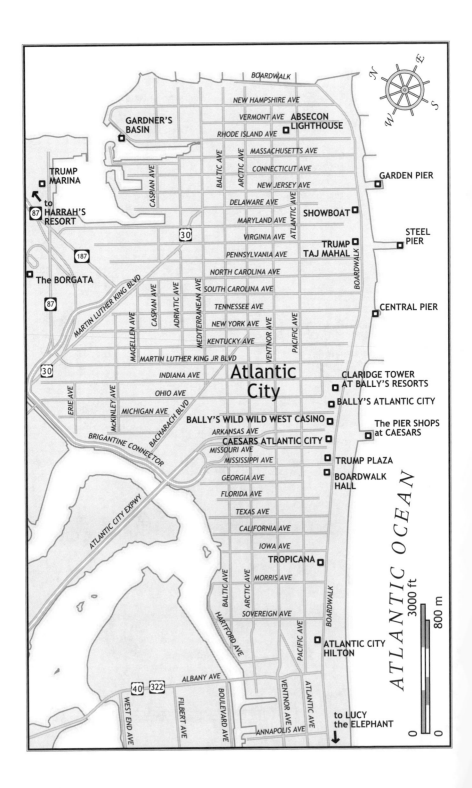

For Emily

If you like being pushed around, then a ride on an authentic Atlantic City rolling chair is perfect for you! For a per-minute fee, these chairs, accommodating between two and three passengers, will take you to your Boardwalk destination.

Table of Contents

How to Use this Book

Tourist Town Guides® makes it easy to find exactly what you are looking for! Just flip to a chapter or section that interests you. The tabs on the margins will help you find your way quickly.

Attractions are usually listed by subject groups. Attractions may have an address, Web site (🖰), and/or telephone number (☎) listed.

Must-See Attractions: Headlining must-see attractions, or those that are otherwise iconic or defining, are designated with the ⭐ Must See! symbol.

Coverage: This book is not all-inclusive. It is comprehensive, with many different options for entertainment, dining, shopping, etc. but there are many establishments not listed here.

Prices: At the end of many attraction listings is a general pricing reference, indicated by dollar signs, relative to other attractions in the region. The scale is from "$" (least expensive) to "$$$" (most expensive). Contact the attraction directly for specific pricing information.

Atlantic City hosted the Miss America pageant for over 80 years.

Introduction

"Here beauty assembles, but it is ofttimes not the beauty of life. It is the glaring show and tinsel array of society that attracts great numbers..."

- Orville O. Hiestand, on Atlantic City, 1922

Atlantic City is the most famous American casino gambling destination outside of Las Vegas, and with good reason. Not only is it the second most popular gambling hotspot in the U.S. (behind Las Vegas), but its beachfront setting within the most populous region of the United States gives it a very desirable location. With about a dozen high-rise resorts and the country's first oceanside Boardwalk (with a capital "B"), it attracts thousands of people every day, and over 30 million people each year. The original version of the Parker Brothers' classic game, Monopoly, was influenced by its street names, and the annual Miss America pageant was held here for over 80 years. Like Las Vegas, it offers visitors the possibility to win big at slots or blackjack, stay in high-quality suites, and rub elbows with the rich and famous.

Of course, however, Las Vegas it is not. Though its beachfront location is far superior to the desert oasis out west, Atlantic City's limited choices for non-gambling entertainment have given the city a more pessimistic aura since gambling was legalized (to combat decades of declining tourism) in 1976. However, even the most cynical Atlantic City critics and tourists alike have seen drastic improvements in the past several years: the luxurious **Borgata** resort, **Atlantic City Outlets**, **The Quarter** at **Tropicana**, and **The Pier Shops at Caesars** are all contributing to this new wave of tourist improvements. In fact, the moment this book hits the press, chances are good that a new mega-attraction will surface, drawing mass media frenzy – just as the Borgata did in 2003. When that happens, this book will be a history lesson; a chapter in a halfway-completed saga of the rebirth of a city.

Atlantic City is an old city that has seen the greatest ups and the most devastating downs. Today, it is fast, *fast* becoming the vacation destination it used to be during its glorious heyday at the turn of the 20th century. Every moment seems to bring about a new and wonderful change, drawing more tourists, and making the city more diverse and an even better place to vacation. It is still not Las Vegas, but the future looks very bright, indeed.

Atlantic City History

Atlantic City has been a summer vacation destination long before casinos hit the Boardwalk. Located on Absecon Island, a
thin stretch of land on the Atlantic Ocean about ten miles long
and separated from the mainland by six miles of uninhabited
swamp, Atlantic City has been a favorite summertime destination for centuries.

EARLY HISTORY

Long before European settlers claimed the land, it was heavily
forested and served as home for the Lenni-Lenape Native
Americans. Their name for the island, Absegami, means "little
water," indicating the thin expanse of water separating it from
the mainland. The island was largely ignored – even after New
Jersey had attained statehood in 1787 – because it was inaccessible from the mainland except by boat.

By 1800, Jeremiah Leeds was one of the first permanent
resident of the island. Fifty years later, only a few others had
joined his descendants as residents (Leeds himself had died in
the 1830s), and the community grew slowly. As these first years
progressed, the name of the island was changed to Absecum,
then later to Absecon.

It was Dr. Jonathan Pitney, a recent graduate of a prestigious
New York college, who saw the future of Absecon Island
as a major tourist destination. By 1852, he and a group of
businessmen had secured the rights to build the Camden-
Atlantic Railroad, which would stretch from Camden, a city
near Philadelphia, to Absecon Island. When naming this new
destination, Richard Osborne, a railway engineer who helped

design the city's basic layout, called it "Atlantic City." Osborne and Pitney together also designed the new city's streets; roads heading north-south would be named after bodies of water (Pacific, Baltic, Mediterranean, etc.), and roads heading east-west would be named after states (Tennessee, South Carolina, Pennsylvania, etc.).

EARLY TOURISM

Atlantic City was incorporated in March of 1854. That same year, the first train made its way down the new line. The total trip of about 60 miles took 2.5 hours, but by the trip's end, as the first vacationers stepped off the train and onto the beach, the era of Atlantic City tourism had begun.

After 1860, Atlantic City became one of the hottest vacation destinations in America. Its primary draw – location – made it accessible from several major urban areas, particularly Philadelphia. People from all over would flock to the city's beaches to enjoy summer activities. At the time, Atlantic City focused on being a "health resort." Doctors would even prescribe the city's "sea air" as a remedy for stress, pain, and even insanity. As the population and tourism grew, businesses began to expand and move closer to the beach.

There became one problem with vendors' close proximity to the beach – the beach itself. Merchants were constantly dealing with beach sand being deposited inside their establishments. In the late 1860s, railroad worker Alex Boardman proposed a solution. Along with others, he suggested a walkway that would rise above the sand and allow beachgoers to clean their feet before leaving the beach. On June 26, 1870, the plan was realized – a wooden walkway that separated the beach from the rest of the city was completed. Boardman's Walk – as it was called – was the world's first. The name was eventually shortened to "Boardwalk." Plus, as an official Atlantic City "street," Boardwalk was (and still is) always spelled with a capital B.

As demand for additional beachfront space rose, the Boardwalk grew. This expansion led to the invention of another Atlantic City staple, the rolling chair, in 1844. A canopied chair designed to be pushed from behind, it made traveling the length of the ever-expanding Boardwalk easier for wealthy vacationers.

Boardwalk real estate became a prime location. All sorts of beachside attractions sprang up, from amusement piers to sideshows to performance theaters to small vendors selling Salt Water Taffy (another Atlantic City first) and more. **Steeplechase Pier, Steel Pier, Heinz Pier**, **Million Dollar Pier**, and others made their debuts in those first few decades of rapid development. At Heinz Pier, starting in the late 1890s, visitors would get a free Heinz Pickle Pin. These pins are still being given out today at the **Atlantic City Historical Museum**.

Between 1890 and 1940, Atlantic City was at its best: presidents came to speak, magicians dazzled audiences, amusement piers came and went and came again, and countless other bits and pieces of history were made. Atlantic City had razzle-dazzle, craziness, in-your-face showiness, corporate enterprise, and everything in between.

The first picture postcards in the U.S. were views of Atlantic City in 1872. Salt Water Taffy was invented and named there around 1880. The first air-conditioned theater opened in the summer of 1896. Although Chicago holds fame for producing the first "Ferris Wheel," it was in 1891 that Williams Somers built an "observational roundabout" on the Boardwalk. It was this wheel ride that was observed and improved upon by George Washington Gale Ferris for the 1893 Chicago World's Fair, and it is his name, not Somers', that is today attached to the ride.

The string of "firsts" continued into the 20th century. In 1915, the first non-subsidized public transportation system, the Atlantic City Jitney, was established. Of course, the Miss America pageant started here in 1921, and continued here for decades. The first official convention hall opened its doors in Atlantic City in 1929. For golfers, the slang terms "Eagle" and "Birdie" were first used here. All this time, the city's tourism was thriving. Every year, more and more people came to visit the city and partake in its glaring show.

THE MISS AMERICA ORGANIZATION

(missamerica.org) One of the most famous events to have taken place on a regular basis in Atlantic City was the annual Miss America Pageant. The first "Miss America" was Margaret Gorman of Washington, D.C., who was crowned in 1921, and after that there was a competition every year until 1927. But when the Great Depression hit, the pageant went into hiatus for several years, while Boardwalk Hall was constructed.

The first depression-era pageant was held in 1933, which was also the first pageant held in Boardwalk Hall. Since then, there have been a few years that lacked a Miss America, and 2003 was the occasion of the 75th crowning. The locals would watch the pageant events with avid interest, and in the weeks leading up to the finals, the city itself would be all dressed up.

However, in recent years the pageant has pulled itself out of Atlantic City, and the 2006 Miss America was crowned in Las Vegas, Nevada. Though Miss America is not necessarily finished with Atlantic City, the tide is definitely turning.

Today, signs of the pageant can still be seen all over the city. Visitors will notice the street name "One Miss America Way," in addition to countless signs and billboards touting this event.

The Miss America Organization is officially a scholarship competition for women between the ages of 17 and 24. The organization gives out about $45 million annually in scholarship and assistance money. Though scholarships are awarded at various levels of the competition (not just in the finals), the actual title of "Miss America" is bestowed upon one woman each year. Being Miss America is actually a job unto itself – it requires extensive traveling throughout the year-long tenure to support various organizations, charities, and other worthy causes.

Atlantic City has historically taken great pride in hosting Miss America. Though the pageant has moved from Atlantic City, and the main offices have also been relocated, many names and places continue to pay tribute to it as one of America's most famous institutions. Many historic remnants of this once vity-defininh event still remain. There is even a small Miss America museum inside the Sheraton hotel.

DOWNFALL OF THE GOLDEN AGE

By 1944, the Atlantic City Boardwalk stretched a staggering seven miles down the coast of Absecon Island – ending in Longport, three cities south. However, in the fall of that year, a massive east coast hurricane destroyed most of the Boardwalk, many attractions, and several amusement piers. The Boardwalk would eventually be rebuilt to a shorter distance of about 5.75 miles (including the Ventnor section).

The hurricane of 1944 may have been the straw that broke the proverbial camel's back for Atlantic City tourism. Commercial airline travel, popularized in the 1930s and 1940s, was making exotic destinations (such as Florida and the Bahamas) more accessible. There was less need for a local vacation destination, and Atlantic City tourism began its steady decline. By the 1960s, Atlantic City was all but dead. With almost no tourist income, high unemployment, and low population, something had to be done.

THE NEW FACE OF ATLANTIC CITY

In 1970, a bill was introduced to the New Jersey Assembly suggesting the statewide legalization of gambling as a way to boost Atlantic City's economy. The bill was rejected and the idea dropped, partly due to pressure from protest groups who were against the idea of legalized gambling in New Jersey. At that point, the only state in the U.S. with legalized gambling was Nevada (established in the 1930s). Three similar gambling bills were brought to the assembly before it was finally approved in 1976, and only after the bill was modified to allow for gambling exclusively in Atlantic City, and not statewide as the previous proposals had suggested. A mere 18 months later, in May 1978, the first casino in Atlantic City – **Resorts International** – opened its doors. In the ensuing years, other casinos quickly followed suit, and the new wave of tourism began.

Legalizing gambling in Atlantic City was meant to revitalize an economically and socially stagnant area. Since 1976, revenues and tourism have skyrocketed, from virtually no tourism to well over 30 million visitors each year. The money generated from gambling was intended, in part, to be invested into the community, as dictated in the Casino Control Act of 1977. For years, however, little progress was made in the way of the city's revitalization. Until recently, it appeared that the casino revenue went right back into the resort. Now, however, things may be changing, as more non-gambling attractions are introduced, and public works are improving slowly but steadily.

Atlantic City History

Gambling was legalized in Atlantic City in the year 1976.

Area Orientation

For many in the Northeast, summer is synonymous with the Jersey Shore. From Sandy Hook to Cape May, New Jersey has turned its Atlantic shoreline into an almost non-stop cavalcade of vacation destinations. From the picturesque southern tip of Cape May to amusement park-crammed Wildwood to the gambling hotspot of Atlantic City, the Jersey Shore is visited by millions of vacationers every year. The variety of activities is endless, with something for just about everyone.

Geographically, the Jersey Shore is a series of many beaches and long, thin islands that run down the eastern coast of the state. Much of these islands are marshland, but the section about a half mile from the coast is packed with motels, private homes, and various beach and amusement attractions. Many of these towns have their own unique boardwalk that separates the beach from the rest of the city. These boardwalks may be lined with shops, arcades, amusement piers, casinos, or private residences. Because the Shore is largely the same throughout the 127-mile stretch, most people do not visit the entire length; they usually have one specific, favorite spot which they visit year after year.

In general, the Jersey Shore is densely crowded during the summer and becomes almost a series of ghost towns in the winter. The exception to this, of course, is Atlantic City, where most of the attractions are indoors, and tourists visit year-round. If you plan on enjoying the beach, perhaps you'd better visit some other Shore destination in the summertime, since Atlantic City's beach, though free to access, isn't as well-kept as other Shore beaches. But if you are looking to enjoy a resort experience with restaurants, casinos, spas, shopping, and more, then Atlantic City is for you, at any time of the year.

GETTING INFORMATION

The more you know about Atlantic City before you go, the more you can do, and the more fun you'll have. Not only will you better appreciate your vacation, the anticipation of seeing the sights will be that much greater. Atlantic City is well-known and generally well-covered, so informations shouldn't be too hard to find.

A.C. CONVENTION AND VISITORS AUTHORITY

(☎ 888.228.4748 🖱 atlanticcitynj.com) The Atlantic City Convention and Visitors Authority can be a great resource when planning your Atlantic City vacation. This special branch of the Chamber of Commerce is dedicated to promoting tourism. While the Authority favors business promotion, it contains a wealth of information both at their physical location and online.

Promotional booklets and fliers containing area information (which are oftentimes full-color and beautifully designed) are usually funded by the businesses themselves and the Authority. Therefore, information obtained via these sources is biased, but it still offers up enough details to give visitors a thorough idea of the Atlantic City's offerings.

INDEPENDENTLY PRINTED TRAVEL GUIDES

With few exceptions, printed travel guides tend to offer a lot more information than the vacationer needs, which may result in over-complicated vacation planning. Certain high-profile destinations such as Las Vegas and Orlando have many books devoted to them. Atlantic City, on the other hand, tends to be covered in books about New Jersey as a whole, or in books about the Jersey Shore. Most popular New Jersey travel guides will have information on Atlantic City.

TRAVEL AGENTS

Commercial travel agents make planning vacations a breeze. They can search for the best deals, book flights and hotels, make restaurant reservations, and even make special requests on your behalf. Their most important asset, however, is their personal knowledge of the destination. They can recommend places to stay and things to see and do like no book or Web site ever could.

However, their service comes with its own price tag, which can be avoided by simply doing your own research – travel agents have no real greater power than a well-informed customer; they just have access to the right information.

THE INTERNET

Travel information constantly changes, and the Internet is a great way to keep up. Unfortunately, because of the largely level playing field of Web sites, it is hard to know which sites to trust and which sites to examine with a bit more skepticism.

A definitive Internet source cannot be offered here; the best advice in learning about your destination of choice would be to (1) check multiple Internet sources, including promotional sites, online travel agencies, and sites with user comments, and (2) check the "official" site, if any – official, meaning the site owned by the attraction or city you are interested in.

SEASONS

As repeat visitors soon realize, there is little to differentiate seasons in Atlantic City, other than the seasonal opening or closing of a few sporadic attractions, like outdoor amusement piers. One could successfully argue that there are only two seasons in Atlantic City – summer and any other time.

SUMMER

(Average High: 83°F, Average Low: 66°F) Atlantic City was historically built for summertime fun. Today, however, the free-access beach is not nearly up to the quality of other Jersey Shore beaches, but during the hottest summer days, people gather their swimwear and head for a dip. Some of the resorts get into the beach action too by creating makeshift "beach bars." Summer is the most popular season, and the outdoor attractions (though few and far between) are up in full swing.

WINTER

(Average High: 45°F, Average Low: 25°F) The temperature drops well below freezing, but the warm comfort of a casino resort is as big a draw as ever. Sure, the crowds dwindle a bit and bargains are more likely, but the resorts are always hopping – especially on New Year's Eve, one of the most crowded days of the year.

SPRING AND FALL

(Average High: 70°F, Average Low: 50°F) There is little downtime or fluctuation in crowds to the casinos, but since Atlantic City is not a true beach resort, many find no reason to visit during the hottest or coldest days, and instead opt for a spring or fall trip. Many of the outdoor attractions are open during at least some part of the spring and fall. If you want to plan your trip around a specific outdoor activity and wish to visit in the off season, please call ahead to make sure that activity will be available during your visit.

PACKING FOR YOUR TRIP

It's not hard to find the essentials in Atlantic City. Still, it is important to plan a bit ahead for the time of year and the attractions you want to visit. There isn't a shortage of gift, sundry, or clothing shops in Atlantic City. This section provides some tips on packing the right items for your vacation. But don't worry; if you do end up forgetting something, chances are you can buy a cheap one in town.

CLOTHES AND TOILETRIES

Of course, pack to reflect your destination and your plans! Atlantic City is on the Atlantic Ocean, so wintertime is freezing and summertime can be very hot (sometimes 90°F or more). Summertime rain and wintertime snow are common as well. The casinos and hotels are climate-controlled, so plan accordingly if you intend to spend most of your time indoors. Many resorts in Atlantic City have laundry-cleaning capabilities; using them may reduce your overall luggage.

Basic toiletries are cheap and small and widely accessible here, so even if you do forget something, in many cases they might be cheap to replace, or even free – many hotels offer free toiletry items (razors, toothbrushes, etc.) to guests upon request.

MEDICATIONS AND OTHER ITEMS

Make sure you have all necessary medications with you before leaving home. Remember to keep important medications close to you at all times. Also, don't forget sunscreen, camera, film and batteries, bathing suit, sunglasses, contact lenses, warm coat, rain jacket, waist pack, purse, long socks, a nice set of clothes (for a nice dinner), packed food for munching, driver's license or photo identification (or passport if you are a non-U.S. citizen), and whatever else your vacation may call for.

GETTING TO ATLANTIC CITY

Atlantic City's close proximity to several large population centers has been a major factor in its development as a vacation destination. Washington, D.C. is about 180 miles away. New York City is about 130 miles away. Philadelphia is a mere 60 miles away. If you don't plan on driving, the Atlantic City International Airport, with services from several major airline carriers, is less than ten miles away. Atlantic City is very friendly towards private bus charters (most resorts have a bus terminal on property) so taking a bus is a great and inexpensive alternative to driving.

FROM POINTS NORTH

Atlantic City is best accessed via the Garden State Parkway in New Jersey. The Parkway is easily reached from various southbound routes, particularly I-95 if your starting point is either New York City or north. In any case, connect to the Parkway heading south as soon as it becomes available. This major highway winds down the east coast of the state and is the main thoroughfare for accessing most points along the Jersey Shore.

Frequent travelers of the Parkway either love it or hate it. It requires several toll stops, and sometimes it can be extremely crowded (especially during the summer months when the Jersey Shore is bustling with activity), but it is a well-maintained and attractive stretch that has a very forested look (especially to anyone leaving the congested Jersey Turnpike/I-95 area around New York City). The mile markers on the Parkway count down to 0 (ending at Cape May, the southern tip of the state), and the Atlantic City Expressway is at exit/mile 38.

FROM POINTS EAST AND SOUTH

Traveling from Philadelphia is simply a matter of negotiating your way onto the Atlantic City Expressway and then holding tight for about 60 miles until you reach the Boardwalk. This expressway is approximately along the original route of the location of the first railroad heading to Atlantic City. Atlantic City is the closest shore point to Philadelphia, which is a primary reason that it exists today. As a result, most traffic comes in and out of the city via this expressway. For Philadelphians, however, speed to the Shore is traded for the more scenic route that upstate vacationers have. The tolled Atlantic City Expressway is simply a matter of getting to the Shore, with little diversion along the way.

Cape May on the southern tip of New Jersey is a dead end. Without taking a 70-plus-minute ferry or driving the long way around the Delaware Bay, you cannot access the Garden State Parkway or Atlantic City. So the best option is to find your way to the Atlantic City Expressway. This is easiest to access via I-95, which runs all the way up and down the east coast of the country (from Maine to Miami). After connecting to the

Atlantic City Expressway from I-95, the drive is an additional 50 miles east to the Boardwalk.

TAKING THE BUS

If you live in a major urban area, such as New York City or Philadelphia, you may have the option of using one of several bus lines' casino express services, such as those offered by **Greyhound** (☎ *800.229.9424* 🖱 *greyhound.com)*. Private bus companies offer greatly reduced fares on a round-trip casino bus ticket, and even a casino bonus (generally equitable to cash) upon arrival. Though these casino bus routes are geared towards gamblers, you do not actually have to gamble. Plus, because of the city's layout, much is accessible by walking directly from the Boardwalk resorts, so you may not even need a car! Of course, a car is a necessity if you wish to explore the surrounding area (and some of the more distant attractions in this book), or don't want to spend a good portion of your day walking up and down the two-plus mile Boardwalk resort area.

Bus service to Atlantic City casinos varies depending on the departure city. There may be five buses a day or one every 15 minutes. In New York City (from Port Authority Bus Terminal), there can be as many as 30-40 buses a day, so you can go to Atlantic City almost whenever you want. If you live in a major urban area (particularly New York City, but also Philadelphia, Washington, D.C., or Baltimore, Maryland), check with your local bus service to see what kind of casino packages they offer. With the proper research and combination of low fares and casino bonuses, people can get round-trip tickets to Atlantic City for as little as $10-$15.

BY AIR

A mere ten miles from the Boardwalk via the Atlantic City Expressway is **The Atlantic City International Airport** *(Egg Harbor Township ☎ 609.645.7895 🖱 acairport.com, airport code: ACY)*. The airport services several popular commercial airlines, as well as charters and even a heliport. Taxi and shuttle services may be available to bring you to the resort area. In addition, there are rental car agencies located within the airport, including Hertz, Avis, and Budget.

BY TRAIN

Those traveling from Philadelphia can use the Atlantic City Line of the **New Jersey Transit** *(🖱 njtransit.com)* to reach the Shore with minimal hassle. The Atlantic City train station is within walking distance to the Boardwalk and the Midtown resort area (but there are frequent resort shuttles available). The station is attached to the new Atlantic City Convention Center and right across the street from the **Sheraton Hotel** *(2 Miss America Way ☎ 609.344.3535)* – the largest non-casino hotel in Atlantic City, which caters to conventioneers.

The **Atlantic City Express Service** *(🖱 acestrain.com)*, operated by the New Jersey Transit, is an "express" train service from New York City to Atlantic City, with one stop in Newark. Even though ACES is more expensive than the bus, the trip takes about 30 minutes longer than by bus or car (sometimes longer if there are track issues, such as snow). The seats are more spacious on the train, and food is available for purchase on board. Still, New Yorkers wishing to take the train no longer have to transfer when going to Atlantic City.

GETTING AROUND ATLANTIC CITY

A majority of the resorts are located on a two-mile stretch of the Boardwalk, directly on the beach of the Atlantic Ocean. So walking between these resorts is a very common practice, especially in the summer. But if a long beachfront walk is not your thing, or if you want to explore beyond the Boardwalk resorts, you're going to need to secure some kind of transportation alternative to your walking shoes.

BY CAR

If you have a car, all resorts have extensive indoor parking garages (many charge a daily-use parking fee of about $5, and sometimes you can even use several resorts' garages for one daily fee).

Driving between Boardwalk resorts is accomplished via either Atlantic Avenue or Pacific Avenue, which parallels the beach. Traffic on these roads can be heavy especially during peak travel times, but since the distances between resorts are not very far, it's generally easy to reach your destination. For resorts in the Marina District, the Atlantic City Connector, accessible right off the Atlantic City Expressway, is the easiest way to go back and forth between resort areas. If you are exploring non-resort areas, much of the city is on a grid. However, in the northernmost section of the city, near **Gardner's Basin**, some streets run diagonal, so a navigational map might be necessary.

ATLANTIC CITY JITNEY

(201 Pacific Ave. ☎ 609.344.8642 🖰 jitneys.net) The Atlantic City Jitney Association was established in 1915, and is currently the longest-running mass transportation company in the United

States that is not government-subsidized. The company operates small, 13-passenger motor coaches that make regular stops at the city's more popular tourist destinations, including all the resorts, the **Absecon Lighthouse**, the NJ Transit Railroad Station, **Gardner's Basin**, City Hall, the library, as well as the hospital and police station. The Jitney is very popular and stops very frequently 24 hours a day, seven days a week.

Jitney routes are color-coded and all routes intersect Pacific Avenue, so you should have little trouble finding the right route along this well-beaten path. Your hotel or resort host will have information about where to access the Jitney, and about routes and destinations. The Jitney fare is $2.25 per single ride (payable in cash only upon boarding), but you can purchase bulk frequent-rider tickets and save a few cents.

TRAVELING BY TAXI

Atlantic City public taxis are abundant, particularly at the major resorts and attractions. Taxi fares are expensive, but if you travel within the city limits, the fare has a cap (of at least $10), so you will not have to spend more than that (most taxi fares around town will wind up being at the cap). Taxis can also be taken from the Atlantic City Airport and other areas.

ROYAL ROLLING CHAIRS

(114 S. New York Ave. ⏾ rollingchairs.com) Though Royal Rolling Chairs is a newer company (established in 2002), traveling on the Boardwalk by rolling chair is almost as old as the Boardwalk itself, and is as much a staple of the city's history as it is a fun and convenient way to get around the Boardwalk. For a per-minute fee, up to three guests at a time can literally be pushed around on small, enclosed chairs as they are calmly brought to their Boardwalk destination. Though not much faster than walking (the chairs are, after all, pushed) they allow you to sit and enjoy the sites. The rolling chairs also operate year-round, with small plastic screens shielding the riders from the winter winds.

TOTAL EXPRESS SHUTTLE

(🖱 harrahs.com) If you are a gambler and want to access only the four Harrah's-operated resorts (**Bally's**, **Caesars**, **Harrah's**, and **Showboat**), then Harrah's offers free shuttle service via the Total Express Shuttle. Contact a Harrah's representative for information on shuttle locations and schedules. Although the Total Express buses are nice and comfortable, the service is very limited. The Atlantic City Jitney, although less comfortable, is much more speedy, frequent, and efficient, and serves *all* resorts plus many other area attractions.

THINGS TO SEE AND DO

Atlantic City is unique in a way that separates it from most other gambling destinations – it did not get its start from gambling. In fact, people flocked to the seaside city long, *long* before gambling was a gleam even in the eyes of Las Vegas (Las Vegas was incorporated in 1911, gambling was legalized there in 1931). They would come from miles around to stroll along the Boardwalk, lie on the beach, and enjoy summer life. So Atlantic City is not historically a gambling town; gambling is a very recent occurrence.

Atlantic City is the only area on the Jersey Shore that sees many tourists consistently year-round. The casinos – the main draws – are entirely indoors. However, many of the non-casino-based activities are open year-round, so a trip to Atlantic City can be fun whenever you plan on visiting.

CASINOS

Casino gambling, of course, is the most popular entertainment option in Atlantic City. But casinos all have a similar appearance, from here to Las Vegas and everywhere in between. They are basically huge rooms filled with slots, table games, bars, and special parlors for high-limit gamblers. Craps, blackjack, roulette, baccarat, and poker are staples of table games, and slot machines offer every imaginable way of spinning wheels to match symbols. Sure, casinos are popular and can be fun, but they don't really make Atlantic City unique.

CASINO OPERATIONS

The **Casino Control Act** is largely responsible for the way Atlantic City operates today. Many of the activities and cultural attractions available to visitors exist almost exclusively because of this addendum to the New Jersey state law. The Act dictates how gambling funds are distributed and how casinos should operate. Those who enjoy Atlantic City's cultural activities, entertainment, and historical monuments should be aware that gambling revenues largely influence their preservation and development. The Casino Control Act functions as follows:

The New Jersey Constitution expressly says that the state is in charge of the gambling in Atlantic City. To that effect, the Casino Control Act created the **New Jersey Casino Control Commission** *(Tennessee Ave. & Boardwalk, Atlantic City* ☎ *609.441.3799* 🖥 *state.nj.us/casinos)*. The commission has been charged with the regulation of gambling within New Jersey and Atlantic City specifically. The office is in charge of licenses, employment, permits, and other issues pertaining to casino gambling. Casino Control Commission offices are located in each of the casino resorts in Atlantic City on the casino floor, and are readily accessible for walk-in information or complaints. The **New Jersey Department of Gaming Enforcement** *(P.O. Box 047, Trenton ✆ njdge.org),* a division of the Office of Law & Public Safety, ensures that the laws and regulations set forth by the state and commission are met.

According to the Casino Control Act, in order to operate a casino within Atlantic City, the following conditions apply: The casino must operate in a hotel with at least 500 rooms of 325 square feet per room or more, which allows for a maximum of 60,000 square feet of gaming space. For each additional 100 rooms, the casino floor may expand 10,000 square feet, up to a total of 200,000 square feet. The hotel must be, in the words of the Casino Control Act, a "superior, first-class facility of exceptional quality which will help restore Atlantic City as a resort, tourist and convention destination." In addition, the commission has the authority to alter the rules of any casino game, including dictate odds, set bet sizes, or change the payout structure.

Atlantic City's casinos gross around $40 million each and every month of the year. Much of this money goes back into the maintenance of the resorts, but a portion must be invested in the economy of New Jersey. This is the job of the **Casino Reinvestment Development Authority** *(1014 Atlantic Ave.* ☎ *609.347.0500).* Created in 1984, the Authority is designed to utilize casino revenue to "give back" to the community by initiating various projects and to create public confidence in the value of casino gambling.

Such projects of the CRDA include partnerships with the **Ocean Life Center**, the **Absecon Lighthouse**, and the **Korean War Memorial**. Various neighborhoods in Atlantic City and the rest of New Jersey have received help from the CRDA. It is through many of these projects and partnerships that Atlantic City has made a major comeback in recent years, in terms of both the local community and the tourism business.

The Casino Control Act also provides compulsive gamblers or those who feel they have a gambling problem the opportunity to be voluntarily placed on an exclusion list. Called the **Self-Exclusion Program**, participants may elect to place themselves on a list distributed to the casinos, which would prevent them from gambling for a specified period of time. Those on the list cannot collect winnings, receive complimentary items from casinos, or apply for casino credit.

To the credit of the Casino Control Act and its creators, Atlantic City has seen a sudden boom in commerce and a second life. The progress has been slow but steady, and most years see an increase in tourism and activities. One day Atlantic City may be known not just for tourism and gambling, but for the local community as well.

Today, the ten-mile stretch of Absecon Island is home to several communities. In addition to Atlantic City, the island also supports the Margate, Ventnor, and Longport communities. Though these communities do not have the same historical prominence or commercial draw of Atlantic City, they have all at some point contributed to – or benefited from – Atlantic City's astonishing success. The main hub of commerce on the island is still the Boardwalk; over 30 million visitors make their way to Atlantic City every year.

BEACH AND BOARDWALK

The defining characteristic of Atlantic City is its beautiful seaside location – it's what Atlantic City was named for, and the reason it exists at all! Though most people don't come to swim, access to the beach is very generous; you can walk right up to the ocean from one of many access points along the Boardwalk. You can sunbathe or swim, but keep in mind that this beach is largely lifeguard-free, so you will probably be on your own. The beach is regularly cleaned and maintained, but not as well as many other Jersey Shore destinations. However, unlike other parts of the Shore, access to Atlantic City's beach is always free!

The Atlantic City Boardwalk lines about six miles of beach. The main resort section populates only a two- to three-mile stretch of this famous walk. In between them are countless small souvenir shops, video arcades, and various food and gift stands. Many hotels also have outdoor bars that are open during nicer weather. As is to be expected, a vast majority of the attractions in Atlantic City are located on the Boardwalk.

RESORT HOTELS

Atlantic City is home to about a dozen large resort hotels, each with its own unique flair. They all have multiple dining options, entertainment and shopping opportunities, and most have some kind of performance venue or convention hall. Eight of the resorts are located on the Boardwalk and the remaining three are in the nearby Marina District. And of course, they all have large casinos.

AMUSEMENT CENTERS

Like California's shoreline, the Jersey Shore is famous for its amusement piers – attractions stretching out onto the beach and sometimes even over the ocean. The Shore has many such piers; some large and well known, others smaller and more intimate. But they all offer much the same experience – a stroll down the Boardwalk with cotton candy and stomach-churning, thrill-inducing midway rides.

In Atlantic City today, there are a total of four amusement piers. Historically, however, there have been many more piers that have come and gone in the early decades of the 1900s. **Heinz Pier** and **Steeplechase Pier** have gone the way of the winds, but The Million Dollar Pier (today **The Pier Shops at Caesars**), **Central Pier** (on the spot of the nation's first amusement pier), and **Steel Pier** have stood the test of time, albeit undergoing repairs and major restorations over the years.

ENTERTAINMENT AND SPORTS

Atlantic City features several sports venues. **Boardwalk Hall**, miniature golf, and outdoor pavilions are available, and all of these are right within your grasp in Atlantic City. Freeskate in a year-round, indoor ice-skating facility. Enjoy concerts, conventions, or play mini-golf directly on the Boardwalk. For those that would like to play a round of "real" golf, the Atlantic City area has many golf courses, public and private, both for daily use and for members only.

PARKS AND RECREATION

In addition to the beach and the ocean, there are other places to relax – and get back to nature – in Atlantic City. **The New Jersey Pine Barrens** is just around the corner, and the **Wharton State Forest** is New Jersey's largest state forest. Just a few miles inland, you can enjoy a hike, canoe ride, camping trip, bike ride, picnic – just about anything you can imagine doing in the Great Outdoors.

For coastal bird-watching and habitat exploration, the **Edwin B. Forsythe National Wildlife Refuge** is the perfect place to visit. And it's also only a short drive up the coast from Atlantic City. If you're more into aquatic exploration, **Gardner's Basin** is a departure point for several area day boat cruises, which may include fishing or sightseeing expeditions. Lakes Bay, part of the marshy expanse that separates island from mainland, is a windsurfer's paradise.

SHOPPING

The Atlantic City area is packed with shopping possibilities, both within the major resorts and outside. From retail department stores to small gift shops to outlet malls and everything in between, chances are you'll find what you're looking for in one of the area's many shopping centers.

Some resorts offer plentiful shopping opportunities, and some even house entire retail malls. But there is much to buy beyond the Boardwalk, with establishments ranging from quaint shopping villages to large outlet malls. Outisde of gambling, shopping is one of the most popular activities in Atlantic City.

NIGHTLIFE

After the day draws to a close, prepare for your night-owl nature to take over. All casinos are open 24 hours a day and several of the resorts host dance clubs and 24-hour restaurants. Atlantic City's nightlife is both famous and infamous, so venture off the Boardwalk to find some key Jersey Shore hotspots and clubs where the party lasts all night.

WHERE TO STAY

When deciding to spend the night in Atlantic City, there is one critical question you must ask yourself: *will you be staying on-resort or off-resort?* There are two worlds to the Atlantic City vacation experience – on one side there are huge resort-hotels, and on the other side there is the rest of the city. There are clear disadvantages and advantages to each class of accommodation, so make sure you know what you are getting into before booking a room.

ON-RESORT

If you are staying on-resort, chances are you'll be paying top-dollar for your room, which may cost upwards of $400 on a busy summer weekend (but can cost as low as $50 if you shop around off-season). You'll be in a higher-quality resort, large and clean, with a collection of on-site restaurants and shops. You'll probably be in a prime location, most likely on the Boardwalk. Of course, directly within your hotel will be a large, clean, and always bustling casino. You may not need a car to get around or enjoy your vacation, since there will be much to do well within walking distance. Additionally, resort-hotels offer many levels of suites. Some have fitness centers, a pool, spa, or health facility. which may come at an additional cost.

OFF-RESORT

If you are staying off-resort, the quality, price, and location of your hotel or motel will vary significantly. You will probably not be on the Boardwalk – you may not even be near the Boardwalk. However, your hotel/motel may offer limited shuttle service to the closest resort. You will be paying less for your room, and may have easier access to the off-Boardwalk attractions. The hotel may have a restaurant, pool, health spa, or other amenities on-site, but most do not. Also, rooms off-resort do not fill up as quickly, so they may be a better option for last-minute vacations.

Since Atlantic City's busiest season is the summer, you can save a lot of money by visiting in the wintertime. You won't be able to enjoy some attractions, such as **Steel Pier** (Atlantic City's amusement park), but many other local attractions will be available for your entertainment. On weekends, room prices soar to about three to four times the weekday rate, and sometimes rooms are unavailable in general. During the busiest times (especially summer holidays), even the most aesthetically questionable of motels may be sold out.

Note: Accommodation information in this book is focused primarily on the casino resorts. In my personal experience, I have a a lot more fun in Atlantic City when staying in a casino resort. However, if you do choose to stay in a non-resort hotel, I suggest that you use an online travel agent (see "Booking a Room") for information.

BOOKING A ROOM

There are several ways to book your hotel room. Most chain hotels (including the resorts) have their own Web sites, and you can mostly book online from there. These sites may have special deals or packages not available elsewhere. You can also use travel agents such as **Travelocity** (☎ *888.709.5983* 🖱 *travelocity.com*) or **Hotels.com** (☎ *800.246.8357* 🖱 *hotels.com*). However, if you need specific accommodations, such as suites, it's recommended you call the resort or hotel directly.

WHERE TO EAT

For many vacationers, eating is the highlight of any trip. For others, however, it is merely a short break from whatever the real attraction may be. There are many, many dining possibilities in Atlantic City, often within the resorts themselves.

FAST FOOD

The quickest, cheapest, and generally least healthy eating option is fast food. There are many fast food choices along the Boardwalk, from independent pizza places to chain establishments. Most fast food in Atlantic City is not drive-through, but there is a drive-through **McDonald's** near the the eastern end of the Atlantic City Expressway

BUFFETS

Casinos and large resorts commonly have buffet-style restaurants, where all the food is set out in a communal area, and customers are free to just walk up and take whatever they want. These are all-you-can-eat places, with drinks costing extra.

TRADITIONAL DINING

Table service at its most inexpensive and convenient, casual dining choices exist in many different shapes and sizes.

Appetizer, entrées, snacks, and desserts are often offered. Dress is casual, though individual establishments may have their own requirements. Dining at a casual restaurant may take an hour or more.

Upscale restaurants generally have a finer ambience, more of a dress code, with better food and better service. Enjoying a fine dining restaurant can take several hours because at these places, the ambience and service is as important as the food.

TIPS AND TIPPING

Restaurant servers, bartenders, and the rest of the staff work largely on tips given by customers. As such, their wage is substantially lower than other occupations.

At a full-service restaurant, 15 to 20 percent of the total bill is a standard tip, which must be divided up between the server, bartender, and other personnel. Tipping of the host or maître'd is optional, depending on any special requests made (birthday cakes, special seating, etc.). Tipping at buffets is generally five to ten percent, depending on the amount of work that is done by the server.

LOCAL PUBLICATIONS

There are numerous publications, both online and in print, that are available for South Jersey and Atlantic City information. Check with your hotel reception desk upon arrival for the latest information. Your hotel may even have a conceirge desk that can provide you with area information, show tickets, and other useful amenities.

CONVENTION AND VISITORS AUTHORITY

(🖰 atlanticcitynj.com) One of the best resources for Atlantic City tourism is the **Atlantic City Convention & Visitor's Authority**. With one location on the Atlantic City Expressway (mile marker 2.5) and one on the Boardwalk directly adjacent to Boardwalk Hall, **The Bureau** is a veritable potpourri of various pamphlets, entertainment and resort listings, and many attractions. It is a promotional service with funds provided by both the state of New Jersey and by the advertisers that use The Bureau's services. Similarly, the **Atlantic City Chamber of Commerce** *(1125 Atlantic Ave.* ☎ *609.345.4524* 🖰 *atlanticcitychamber.com)* is closely tied with the Convention & Visitors Authority, with an emphasis on promotion as opposed to tourism.

NEWSPAPERS

For time-specific information about events, concerts, and advertisements pertinent to Atlantic City and the vicinity, there are several local publications available. The largest and oldest free publication in the area is **The Atlantic City Weekly** *(8025 Black Horse Pike, Suite 350, West Atlantic City* ☎ *609.646.4848* 🖰 *acweekly.com)*, which is available throughout the city at various information kiosks, including most resorts and hotels. While the paper contains some local news and current events, these stories are undermined by the plethora of advertisements pertaining to local attractions, touring shows and show times, restaurants, bars, and classifieds.

For a daily print newspaper, the **Press of Atlantic City** *(1000 W. Washington Ave., Pleasantville* ☎ *609.272.4000* 🖰 *pressofatlanticcity.com)* features local and national news stories, as well as classifieds, advertisements, and area information.

The paper offers a subscription, or can be purchased at a local newsstand.

The Atlantic City Boardwalk was the first boardwalk in the country, and most of the city's attractions are contained within its two-mile stretch.

Garden Pier

Lucy the Elephant in Margate

Resting by the dunes on the beach

Looking out over the beach from The Pier Shops

Indoor pool at The Water Club

The first slot machine in Atlantic City on display at Resorts

The water show at The Pier Shops

Bench on the Boardwalk

The Renault Winery

Historic Smithville

Roman columns at Caesars

Iconic Atlantic City life boat

While many of the resorts on the Boardwalk were built since the gambling age, others are renovated old hotels from the late 1800s and early-mid 1900s.

The Atlantic City Resorts

Most of the main tourist attractions in Atlantic City are located on a two-mile stretch of the world famous Atlantic City Boardwalk (the first boardwalk in the country). On the southern end is the **Atlantic City Hilton** and on the northern end is **Harrah's Showboat**. In this section, we will travel up the Boardwalk through the entire two-mile stretch and explore the area's chief tourist attractions.

The other major resort section of Atlantic City, called the **Marina District**, is home to three resort-hotels that do not have immediate beach access, and can't be gotten to by walking. Major traffic into the Marina District travels from the Boardwalk via the Atlantic City Connector, a short stretch of road which is partially underground. It allows fast, easy access and the ability to bypass the otherwise congested streets throughout the rest of Atlantic City.

Most major traffic into Atlantic City comes from the west on the Atlantic City Expressway, which starts in Philadelphia and stretches all the way to the ocean, with major connections for I-95 and the Garden State Parkway (for points north and in New York).

As visitors arrive on the Atlantic City Expressway, they get a great view of the backs of most of the resorts. Unlike most other types of resorts, those in Atlantic City require that you enter through their back entrance. This is because the fronts of the buildings face the ocean. For many buildings located on the Boardwalk; you will not be able to see the main entrance until you walk out onto the Boardwalk.

Although most of the hubbub revolves around the resorts themselves, there is much to see in the sections between the hotels (small gift shops and video game arcades and even several amusement piers).

CHOOSING YOUR RESORT

If you intend to stay in one of these resort hotels, the task of deciding where to book your reservation may seem daunting. Although most resorts are located within a single two-mile line (and you can easily walk between them, sometimes without even stepping outdoors), where you stay is definitely going to be a factor in how much you enjoy yourself.

Before you cram these pages and nervously make that reservation phone call, know this – all of the resort-casinos listed in this section are of fine quality, and they all have substantial similarities. You're not going to get treated like a king in one and a pauper in another. Each resort has a casino, parking facilities, various kinds of rooms, and several restaurants that cater to diverse palates. However, the resorts vary substantially on beach access, shopping and entertainment possibilities, and (of course) location.

BOARDWALK RESORTS

It is America's first Boardwalk. Since the late 1800s, people have been flocking from all over the east coast to this vacation destination to bask in the sun, walk on the beach, and shop or play on the Boardwalk. It is the centerpiece of Atlantic City, and perhaps (debatably) of the entire Jersey Shore. It is the jewel around which the rest of Atlantic City is built. Of course, the days have changed significantly since those of yore. Casinos have largely replaced the beachside amusements and oddities that once dotted the famous stretch. But still, it is no surprise that today the Boardwalk hosts more of Atlantic City's attractions than any other part of town. If you stay and play on the Boardwalk, you are in the middle of all the action. These resorts have the major advantage of having direct Boardwalk and beach access. In addition, many of the resorts are inter-connected in such a way that you can explore them without ever setting foot outside.

OLD HOTELS AND NEW HOTELS

One of the more interesting and eclectic aspects of Atlantic City is the combination of old and new hotels. While many of the resorts on the Boardwalk were built since the gambling age, others are radically renovated old hotels from the late 1800s and early-mid 1900s, when Atlantic City was in its historical heyday. These old hotels still maintain the exteriors' original charm; much the way it probably looked to the vacationers of yesteryear. Of course, the interiors are all newly remodeled to fit casinos and modern amenities.

One of the original requirements for building a resort casino in Atlantic City was that the resort had to be in a newly built facility. The resorts that are in old renovated hotels (such as **Claridge** and **Resorts**) were able to bypass this rule by making significant updates to the interiors, or by adding new wings and expanding.

It is interesting to see the unique combinations of some of these resorts; since many have been pieced together by upgrades or by acquiring and re-modeling older hotels, there is a non-conformity about more than a few of them. Crossing over from a new edition to an old edition may or may not be noticeable, depending on the quality of the patch-and-paint job and the keenness of a discerning eye.

WHAT TO LOOK FOR

With so many resort choices both on the strip and off the strip, how does one choose where to stay? While the resorts vary on some key points, they are largely similar in the amenities they may offer.

PRICE

Most people start to look at accommodations based on their price; which can vary significantly from resort to resort. Cheap resorts can be *really* cheap, but expensive ones can start at hundreds of dollars per night. Keep in mind, however, that resort prices fluctuate greatly on a seasonal, and sometimes almost daily, basis.

SIZE

Atlantic City resorts are large, and generally range between about 1,000–2,000 guest rooms divided into one or more "towers." The minimum guest-room count to obtain a gambling license in New Jersey is 500, but most resorts more than double this requirement.

CASINO

For those interested in gambling, a large casino can be impressive but very daunting. Moreover, larger casino floors don't tend to have different games, but rather more of the same games. Therefore, a 60,000 square foot casino probably has the same kinds of games as a 100,000+ square foot casino.

Casino loyalty programs are also popular reasons to choose a particular resort. If somebody has complimentary bonuses at a particular hotel or hotel chain, they may wish to visit that casino.

Note: This guide makes reference in a very general way to the gambling facilities available in a given casino. It does not provide specific playing tactics (see the "Casino Games" chapter). Please consult other sources for this information.

FOOD

Gambling is the main attraction in Atlantic City and unfortunately, dining options take a back seat. However, all resorts have several (sometimes more than five or six) dining choices, running the gamut from buffet or cafeteria to upscale fine cuisine. Though there are a few highlights for restaurants in Atlantic City worthy of resort-hopping, visitors can stick to the restaurants in their resort, as they will likely have a fine selection. When applicable, general restaurant price is *roughly* indicated as such: $$$ = fine dining; $$ = casual; $ = fast food.

Not all restaurants have price information in this guide. Bars and lounges generally do not have a price indicator. For more specific or accurate restaurant pricing, contact the resort directly.

SHOPPING

While most resorts have only a basic number of shopping options, mostly gift shops and sundries, there are a few diamonds in the rough. A few resorts have elaborate shopping centers reminiscent of Las Vegas, with many upscale shops featuring clothing, jewelry, accessories, miscellaneous items, and other such merchandise.

POOL, SPA, AND FITNESS CENTER

Unlike Las Vegas (and many other gambling destinations), Atlantic City has a beautiful stretch of Jersey Shore beach. Because of this, the pool and fitness centers in the resorts are less important, and markedly smaller than their desert-location counterparts out west. Nonetheless, each resort has its own fitness center and sometimes even a pool. Access to these facilities may not be included in accommodation price.

SHOWS

Most resorts in Atlantic City have one large entertainment venue or showroom and several smaller venues, often within bars or clubs. Though there are occasionally resident shows in a resort, these are normally off-season, and the resort show-rooms are most often used by traveling performers and tours during their east coast visit.

ATTRACTIONS

Each resort has something about it that makes it unique. In many cases, the theme of the resort will translate into some kind of attraction; be it an on-property museum, video arcade, or other such specialty.

RESORTS: BOARDWALK DOWNBEACH

With only two resorts, the Boardwalk Downbeach section of Atlantic City is the smallest resort area. However, these two resorts are among the best and most popular in the city, and feature upscale accommodations and lots of non-gambling entertainment. Visitors will undoubtedly make their way to the Downbeach section at some point during their visit.

ATLANTIC CITY HILTON

(Boston Ave. & Boardwalk ☎ 609.347.7111 ⛟ hiltonac.com) The southernmost resort on the Boardwalk, at the very end of the resort area, is the Atlantic City Hilton. It is a classy and upscale establishment, and reliant on good old-fashioned quality and customer service rather than casino-resort tackiness to draw visitors. The Hilton is a favorite for those who enjoy a more subdued elegance rather than showiness.

The Atlantic City Hilton has changed names and ownership several times over the years. The site was originally a small motel bought by Las Vegas Golden Nugget casino mogul Steve Wynn in the early 1980s. In no time it was turned into the Atlantic City Golden Nugget and was an instant and overwhelming success. But Wynn was not happy with the strict rules of Atlantic City gambling, so he decided to sell the property to Bally's/Caesars and it was renamed Bally's Grand... and a few waves of a magic wand later, it is now a Hilton.

There are about 800 rooms and a selection of suites available in the Atlantic City Hilton of various sizes. Additionally, the resort received a *AAA Four Diamond Rating,* which is a very rare honor to bestow upon an Atlantic City resort (most other resorts are *AAA Three Diamond*). The rooms here are somewhat larger and nicer, with more amenities than is to be expected from the other resorts.

The Atlantic City Hilton features a smaller casino floor, with about 60,000 feet of gaming space. It is not cramped, however, and has the latest popular slot machines and table games in an upscale and classier gaming environment. It also features an Asian-themed casino area and a poker room.

The Atlantic City Resorts 63

The Atlantic City Hilton has exceptional pool and health spa facilities. The pool is indoors (open year-round), and provides an outdoor sundeck, glass walls, and ceiling for added light and ambience. There is also a significant 13,000-square-foot fitness and spa for both men and women.

TROPICANA CASINO & RESORT

(Brighton Ave. & Boardwalk ☎ 609.340.4000 ☷ tropicana.net) In just a few short years, Tropicana went from being "just another A.C. resort" to being one of the biggest and best resorts in the city. This is mostly due to its attitude toward non-gambling entertainment.

In 2004, Tropicana unveiled a Las Vegas-like shopping and entertainment complex, **The Quarter**, which was at the time unique in Atlantic City. As a whole, Tropicana is a complete destination resort. There is much shopping, dining, playing, and relaxing to do without even stepping foot outside. It is indeed a comprehensive and fun place.

Tropicana'a life in in Atlantic City began when Ramada Corporation announced it was purchasing the Tropicana in Las Vegas, and would build a Tropicana in Atlantic City on the site of the old Ambassador Hotel. The casino first opened in November 1981. About a decade ago, Tropicana became the first hotel in Atlantic City to enhance family-friendliness. The indoor Atlantic City-themed amusement park, "TropWorld," was unsuccessful, and in 1996, it was destroyed to make room for more gaming space.

Tropicana's 2,000 guest rooms make it one of the largest hotels in Atlantic City. The rooms are divided into several different towers, including the newer and more expensive Havana Tower, which is closest to The Quarter complex. Tropicana offers several different levels of suites.

Tropicana's very large casino is spread over several sections on multiple floors. Totaling about 125,000 square feet, the casino seems smaller due to its division of gaming space. It is an attractive and lively place that caters to a wide range of tastes and budgets. Popular table games and slots are represented. The casino also features a poker room.

Tropicana is one of the only resorts in Atlantic City with more than one pool. The hotel features both an indoor and outdoor swimming pool; the indoor one is open year-round. Tropicana also has a complete health club and spa facility, including massages, a hot tub and sauna, as well as various items of fitness equipment.

RESORTS: BOARDWALK MIDTOWN

The bustling and congested Midtown section of the Boardwalk is Atlantic City's most populous; it has the most resorts, the most guest rooms, and the most casino space crammed into one small area along the Boardwalk. It is here that many of most famous casino resorts are located. Its ease of accessibility from the Atlantic City Expressway, famous resort names, and central Boardwalk location make it a very popular place.

TRUMP PLAZA
(Mississippi Ave. & Boardwalk ☎ 609.441.6000
☗ **trumpplaza.com)** Donald Trump's design style for his buildings has always been a kind of over-the-top, gaudy flair, with

everything shiny and gold-plated. As the mid-sized Trump casino, however, Trump Plaza has undergone a bit of a facelift in recent years, toning down a bit of that showy Trump "style" that has become somewhat of a design trademark. Though it is still decidedly Donald, the décor is more contemporary, the casino is a bit classier and subdued, and the rooms are generally nicer.

Still, visitors familiar with Trump will definitely feel at home here. Trump Plaza has gone though several legs of history, including the "Trump World's Fair" casino, and the resort is also Donald Trump's first casino in Atlantic City.

Trump Plaza is actually a combination of one large resort casino and one much smaller casino. The smaller one was initially owned by Playboy Enterprises, but the resort did very poorly. Trump purchased the resort and added it to his Trump Plaza complex, first as a regular resort and finally as a casino in 1996.

The resort features about 900 rooms (in two towers) and various levels of suites. The main tower of Trump Plaza is 39 stories. The resort and the rooms have been recently renovated to reflect a more subdued, contemporary style. The casino floor at Trump Plaza features about 90,000 square feet of gaming space stretched along a long, thin room, glittery with that famous Trump style. It has many favorite slot machines and table games.

Trump Plaza houses the indoor pool and spa facilities. The pool is Olympic-style and one of the biggest in Atlantic City. During the summer an outdoor sundeck is available. The **Plaza Spa** offers several choices for relaxation and spa treatment options, such as hot tubs, steam rooms, and saunas. Swedish and aromatherapy massages and various body treatments are available for an extra charge. Reservations should be made in advance for these services. Tanning beds are also available, as well as a small fitness facility with all the standard workout and cardio equipment typical of a small gym.

CAESARS ATLANTIC CITY

(Arkansas Ave. & Boardwalk ☎ 609.348.4411 📞 caesarsac.com)
Caesars Atlantic City was the second casino to establish itself in Atlantic City, opening in 1979 as Caesars Boardwalk Regency. Although it boasts over 1,200 rooms in four different towers, the resort feels small, organized, and manageable. And unlike many of the other resorts along the Boardwalk, Caesars Atlantic City has maintained its consistent branding (no major name change) of the property, enabling its emergence as one of the best-known and most constant landmarks on the Boardwalk. Harrah's Entertainment owns the Caesars name.

Caesars Palace, the Caesars flagship resort in Las Vegas, is still much bigger and better than this smaller Atlantic City counterpart. However, with the arrival of the much-anticipated **Pier Shops at Caesars**, Caesars Atlantic City has become one of the premier destinations in a city that has been re-inventing itself over the past several years. It has the best location on the Boardwalk, central to much of Atlantic City's entertainment.

Caesars Atlantic City is, divided into four different towers. The oldest are the North and South Temple Towers, and the Ocean Tower. The adjacent Centurion Tower is the newest and nicest. Some Temple Tower rooms have windows overlooking the indoor lobby.

The Atlantic City Resorts

The Atlantic City Resorts

67

The **Temple Lobby** at Caesars is one of the few places in the resort reminiscent of the Roman flair in Las Vegas. On entering the lobby, one gets the feeling of having stepped into the cool twilight of a Roman evening. The dusky ambient lighting evokes a sense of peaceful calm, highlighting a sky-painted ceiling. Artificial torches line the second-floor balconies and scattered oases of palm trees complete the scene.

The casino floor at Caesars Atlantic City is over 120,000 square feet – a larger casino size for Atlantic City. Plus, it is particularly well organized, bright, and easy to navigate; no complicated maze. It features all the latest slot and table games, as well as a poker room. The second-floor casino, which is smaller, has an indoor connecting walkway to the Pier Shops.

Caesars has one small outdoor pool, which is only open during the summertime. Though the pool itself is unimpressive, the adjacent **Qua Baths & Spa**, which has recently been renovated, has many additional amenities, including fitness equipment, hot tubs and saunas, and various spa and massage treatments.

BALLY'S ATLANTIC CITY
(Park Place & Boardwalk ☎ 609.340.2000 ⬤ ballysac.com)

If there was a shing example of mixing old and new hotels in Atlantic City, Bally's Atlantic City would be it. The resort is a collection of re-designed old hotels and new facilities. Specifically, Bally's comprises three separate resorts, which have fused together over the years. Today it is collectively one of the largest resorts in Atlantic City. **Bally's Wild Wild West Casino, Bally's Park Place** (the "main resort"), and

Claridge Casino have combined casino floor areas to create the largest total casino floor space in Atlantic City. Two of the three areas have hotel rooms available – Bally's Park Place and the **Claridge Tower** – adding up to over 2,000 rooms in this massive (and oftentimes confusing) complex with two different fitness/spa/pool areas.

Booking a room at Bally's means your room may be located in one of four different hotel areas: the new Bally's Tower, Garden Tower, or the pre-casino Claridge or Dennis Hotel. Bally's Tower is generally the most upscale, and the Dennis Hotel is the most accessible and least expensive.

Indeed, Bally's offers quite a confusing mix. Inside the casino, it is sometimes difficult to tell which part of the resort you are in - and whether or not you are in an old building or a new building - since they all blend together via a series of indoor windowless walkways. Fortunately, none of this matters much since they all rooms are booked through Bally's central reservation desk, and once you're there, you can explore everything.

As is to be expected, there are many different rooms and suites to choose from, ranging from basic rooms to lavish suites. Bally's added the Claridge resort to its roster of Atlantic City destinations in 2002. Before then, Claridge operated as its own separate casino-resort.

All three resort areas are located side-by-side along the Boardwalk, with Bally's Wild Wild West Casino at the southern end, Claridge Casino at the north, and Bally's Park Place in between. Right next door is **Caesars Atlantic City**, which is also owned by Harrah's Entertainment.

Bally's Park Place, the original resort of the Bally's complex, was the third resort in Atlantic City. Many years later, Park Place Entertainment (now part of Harrah's Entertainment) built The Wild Wild West Casino next door, and ultimately acquired the Claridge to the north.

The resort's total casino space, including all sections, is about 220,000 square feet, making it the largest casino in Atlantic City and larger than any casino in Las Vegas. Plus, Bally's Atlantic City is located right in the middle of the Boardwalk, with easy access to many of the surrounding casinos.

It is also right across from the **Atlantic City Outlets**, near the bus terminal and **The Pier Shops at Caesars**, making it an all-around ideal location. Overall, Bally's Atlantic City is an inexpensive and casual resort, always crowded, and has an unfortunate "run-down" look. Of course, what it lacks in appearance it makes up for in size.

BALLY'S WILD WILD WEST CASINO

(Part of Bally's Atlantic City) Only in a casino resort town can you go from Ancient Rome to the old American West in just a few steps. Bally's Wild Wild West is immediately next to **Caesars Atlantic City** – which is no surprise, since the same company owns them both.

Completed in 1997, Bally's Wild Wild West Casino is perhaps the most thoroughly themed casino along the strip, a fact that's very apparent from both the Boardwalk side and the street side. The exterior is designed to look like a string of "Old West" buildings, painted with bright and pastel colors.

This casino is perhaps the only theme-based casino you will find in Atlantic City that emulates the themes of an average-quality Las Vegas casino. Although other façades in Atlantic City exist mostly in the resort's main entrance and lobby, Bally's Wild Wild West Casino goes all out – each casino room is intricately decorated to resemble a western town during the gold rush; there is a waterfall, a general store, and many old-West-style buildings. It is designed to look like you are outside in the evening, strolling through a neighborhood in the Old West. There are even animatronic western folk that wish you good luck as you gamble or amble.

Bally's Wild Wild West Casino is a winding and confusing casino floor. It totals about 80,000 square feet of gaming space and has many slot and table games in a lively western-style environment. It also has a very large race and sports book. The casino also features a large array of video poker machines and **Coyote Kate's Slot Parlor**.

BALLY'S PARK PLACE

(Part of Bally's Atlantic City) Bally's Park Place is the "main casino" of the Bally's complex. It is home to the large Bally's Tower where most of the resort's overnight accommodations are located, as well as **The Spa at Bally's**. Bally's Park Place was the original resort – **Wild Wild West Casino** was built in 1997 and the **Claridge Tower**, though built in the 1930s, was acquired by Bally's in 2002.

Bally's Park Place was the third casino-resort in Atlantic City. In the late 1970s the company bought and leveled the Marlborough-Blenheim Hotel and renovated the nearby **Dennis Hotel**. However, it barely surpassed the 500-room minimum required for a gambling license. In 1988, Bally's was the first casino to exceed 1,000 rooms with the introduction of

The Atlantic City Resorts

the Tower, which to this day remains one of the most noticeable buildings on the Boardwalk.

Since Bally's Park Place is Bally's main casino, and since Bally's Atlantic City is collectively the largest casino resort in Atlantic City, it is understandable that most of the buses, traffic, and pedestrian thoroughfare converge at Bally's. That, added to its ideal location – right in the middle of the Boardwalk resort area – makes Bally's Park Place one of the most popular resorts in town.

The casino at Bally's Park Place is one huge, square box. This unimaginative shape may bode well for people looking for an easily navigable space, but it lacks the intimacy of casino spaces with more twists and turns. The floor is about 80,000 square feet with many popular slot and table games, and a large race and sports book. Overall, the casino is inexpensive, with low minimum bids and plenty of low-denomination slots.

The Spa at Bally's (★ Must See!) is one of the best pool and spa facilities in Atlantic City. Until the **Borgata** opened and **Harrah's Resort** upgraded its pool area, it was the undisputed king of Atlantic City resort spas. Unfortunately, it is not comparable to the extravagant multi-acre facilities in Las Vegas, but if having a good spa facility is integral to your vacation experience, Bally's is a fine choice.

The Spa at Bally's has a very nice indoor swimming pool and several whirlpools in one central room that is nicely designed with a semi-tropical theme (with plants and few cascading fountains). There are lounge chairs surrounding the pool and private areas for massages and spa treatments.

For sporty attire and accessories, Bally's **Spa Pro Shop** is located right in the spa area. There is even the **Spa Café** within the confines of the spa area, so you can enjoy a quick and healthy bite while you relax the day away and rejuvenate. And the best part is that the indoor facility is open year-round.

CLARIDGE TOWER

(Part of Bally's Atlantic City) The Claridge Hotel, originally built in the 1930s, was renovated for casino use and re-opened in 1981. It is the smallest casino in Atlantic City, a fact that has historically not been very good for business. In 2002 it was purchased by Bally's and renovated yet again as The Claridge Tower at Bally's. Today, The Claridge Casino Hotel is one of the few resorts in Atlantic City that has maintained its original look from the city's heyday (other hotels have either been torn down or extensively re-modeled).

Although it is considered a "Boardwalk Resort," Claridge is not on the Boardwalk. Rather, it is one block away, overlooking **Brighton Park** on the Oceanside, with the view of the Atlantic Ocean further in the distance than most other Boardwalk resorts.

The Claridge Tower has just over 500 rooms, making it the smallest Atlantic City hotel. Claridge rooms are inquired about and booked through the main Bally's Atlantic City office. Sometimes you can choose to stay at Claridge, other times you may have to stay at either **Bally's Tower** or the **Dennis Hotel**, depending on how crowded the hotel is for the night. In either case, if you stay at either Bally's or Claridge, you have access to all the amenities at both places.

Claridge rooms are nice and quaint, while still maintaining a decent size. There are various levels of accommodations here as well as at Bally's main resort, but there are significantly less rooms here. Claridge is also one of the best remodeling jobs in all of Atlantic City – the resort maintains an air of the old charm, but still feels somewhat fresh and new.

Guest rooms and public space in the old Claridge Hotel were converted into the casino at Claridge, which is a very small and intimate space. Twisting through about 60,000 square feet on several floors, the casino features popular slot and table games. Of particular note is **PennyVille**, which has a large selection of penny and nickel slots.

The small but nice indoor pool and fitness area at Claridge is one of the most intimate and comfortable pool areas, which – if not too crowded – can really be relaxing. There are huge windows that let in an abundance of light (especially if it's sunny) and relaxing lounge chairs with decorative trees scattered about. Of course, all the standard massage, spa, and fitness services are available. The fitness room is small but it has most of what is needed to get a good workout.

Though the **Spa at Bally's** (located at **Bally's Park Place**) is one of the best pool and spa areas in Atlantic City, the Claridge's intimate pool environment is a definite plus. The Spa at Bally's is the most popular but also frequently the busiest. Guests of Bally's can use both pools and spas at either Bally's or Claridge.

It is nice to stay at Claridge because of its history and its quiet ambience. Don't expect top-quality rooms. At the north end of the Bally's complex, Claridge makes for a quiet retreat and a smaller, more intimate casino floor.

RESORTS: BOARDWALK UPTOWN

At the north end of the Atlantic City Boardwalk, just before it begins to wind around the northern tip of Absecon Island, is the most secluded resort area on the Boardwalk. In fact, a half-mile of seaside condos, empty lots, and local gift shops separate the Uptown from Midtown sections. However, it is here that three rather large and impressive resorts, **Showboat**, **Trump Taj Mahal**, and **Resorts Atlantic City** can be found. Despite it being the most remote section of the Atlantic City Boardwalk, these resorts offer up some pretty spectacular entertainment and gargantuan guest room counts.

RESORTS ATLANTIC CITY

(1133 Boardwalk ☎ 609.344.6000 ⬢ resortsac.com) When gambling was finally legalized in Atlantic City in 1976, the first casino to open was Resorts International, a mere 18 months later. Investors had purchased the Chalfonte-Haddon Hall Hotel, and instead of building an entirely new resort, only had to do some simple renovations, since the old hotel already met the 500-room minimum requirements.

The original hotel had about 1,000 rooms, but the new ownership cut the rooms down to under 600 to accommodate the casino floor and other on-site amenities. On May 26, 1978, at 10:00 a.m., as Resorts International opened its doors, the gambling era in Atlantic City was born. Over the years, Resorts Atlantic City has had numerous owners, including Donald

Trump and Merv Griffin. It is a complex that holds the unique Atlantic City title of being the first legal casino.

Resorts Atlantic City is the southernmost casino-resort of the Boardwalk's uptown area, and much of the original hotel's façade still exists. It has a classical old look, but it is easy to tell where additions have been made to the original over the years. The design today is a pleasant and colorful art deco, from the exterior to the rooms to the casino floor.

Resorts Atlantic City has about 1,100 guest rooms in two different hotel towers. The classic tower, called the **Ocean Tower**, is part of the original hotel, which sits right on the Boardwalk. The visibly newer **Rendezvous Tower** (which opened in 2004) is 27 stories high and has standard size rooms, hot tub suites, and various other levels of rooms and suites. The Rendezvous Tower has a more contemporary exterior than the Ocean Tower.

The large casino floor at Resorts is about 100,000 square feet and features the latest popular slot and table games. When it opened, the Rendezvous Tower added about 24,000 feet of gaming space. The art deco motif extends throughout, and Resorts' casino has a more pleasant and laidback atmosphere.

Resorts also has an indoor-outdoor pool that is open year-round within its larger spa facility. The resort also has a fitness center, whirlpool, and the other expected spa amenities. They offer massages as well – Swedish, aromatherapy, and more. During summertime, many of the massages can be experienced on an outdoor deck area. Also operating in the summertime is an outdoor bar.

TRUMP TAJ MAHAL

(1000 Boardwalk at Virginia ☎ 609.449.1000 ☏ trumptaj.com)

The third and newest of the three Donald Trump resorts in Atlantic City, Trump Taj Mahal is the most noticeable and largest in the uptown area. With a grand unveiling in 1990, it is also widely considered to be the best of Trump's Atlantic City resorts. In fact, until the **Borgata** was completed in 2003, the Trump Taj Mahal was also the newest resort in Atlantic City – a title it held for 13 years. It is clean, upscale, large, plush, classy, and has among the most devoted regular customers of any resort on the Boardwalk.

Due to the position and size of the building, it is also the most recognizable resort on the Boardwalk, and can be seen from miles away. As the somewhat egocentric name suggests, the Trump Taj Mahal has a stong Indian theme – and is the most intricately themed of all the Trump Resorts. It encompasses over 17 acres of almost entirely enclosed space, and it is one of the tallest buildings in New Jersey. This, coupled with one of the largest casino floors in the country, makes Trump Taj Mahal a monster of a resort.

Trump Taj towers at 51 stories. However, the resort has only 1,200 rooms and suites. In addition to the standard rooms, the Taj offers a variety of themed suites from which to choose. Of particular note are the large and themed hospitality suites.

The casino at Trump Taj Mahal, as is to be expected, is a massive winding maze of popular slot and table games. The floor is about 150,000 square feet, making it the largest single casino in Atlantic City (Bally's is larger but is actually three casinos). The casino also has a poker room and a race and sports book. The poker room is home to the *ESPN United States Poker Championships.*

Available to hotel guests only, Trump Taj Mahal has an indoor pool facility that is open year-round. Additionally, there is a full fitness, spa, and salon center that features all the pampering one would expect. In the summertime, there is also an outdoor sun deck available.

SHOWBOAT ATLANTIC CITY

(801 Boardwalk ☎ 609.343.4000 ⬥ showboatac.com) Harrah's casinos are famous for their perpetual party atmosphere, but Showboat takes this to a whole new level. As one of the livelier casinos on the Boardwalk, Showboat is billed as "The Mardi Gras Casino." It really has a more general New Orleans theme.

The Showboat first opened in 1987. Since Resorts International originally owned much of the property uptown, the land on which Showboat is built has been leased from them. Harrah's purchased the casino much later, in 1998.

Showboat (including the casino floor) is long and thin, which makes it one of the easiest resorts to navigate. As the hotel stretches back, one long side is reserved strictly for casino activity, while the other side has some of the various restaurants and activities.

Showboat used to be one of Atlantic City's smaller resorts, but a slew of recent renovations added an entirely new hotel tower, more entertainment and gaming options, and an entirely new Boardwalk-facing façade. Today, despite its northerly location, Showboat has sprung up in popularity from a sleeper to a real gem of a resort. A major recent addition is the **House of**

Blues, which includes a smaller casino, a few specially-designated rooms, and, of course, a concert venue and restaurant.

Showboat is a pleasant surprise. It has two towers – the tallest being 25 stories – and 1,300 guest rooms and suites. One of the towers opened with the original hotel and the other is the result of a multi-million dollar renovation, which was completed in mid-2003. Showboat comprises several different levels of room styles and well over 200 suites. The cream of the crop among the rooms on offer are the "Super Suites."

The casino floor is long and thin (as is the resort itself), and most major non-gambling activities are located on the sides of the main casino level. As such, the 120,000-square foot casino is fairly easy to navigate, and getting to and from the guest rooms is relatively easy as well. The casino features popular table and slot games and also features a simulcast race facility.

Resort guests also have access to the **Big Easy Spa** and pool facilities. The spa features basic workout equipment and tanning booths, steam baths, hot tubs, saunas, and other amenities (including massages by appointment). The pool is outdoors and thus seasonal. The outdoor deck is small, with little more than a few deck chairs. **Vive Day Spa and Salon** is also available for various beautification requirements (hair, nails, and skin care).

RESORTS: MARINA DISTRICT

Although the Atlantic City Boardwalk is by far the most famous and well-traveled section of the city, there is another area that definitely deserves attention – the Marina District. Specifically, the Marina District is a set of three resort-hotels that do not reside on the Boardwalk. The resorts in the Marina District are: **Trump Marina**, **Harrah's Resort**, and the **Borgata**. Though not interconnected and not as easily accessible as Boardwalk resorts, these are among the nicer resorts in Atlantic City. Even if you plan on spending most of your vacation on the Boardwalk, these resorts are woth checking out.

Getting to the Marina District is easy from the other casinos. Visitors with cars just need to follow the signs. Alternatively, take a taxi or the Atlantic City Jitney. A direct, one-way trip from the Boardwalk to the Marina District by car is about five minutes.

HARRAH'S RESORT

(777 Harrah's Blvd. ☎ 609.441.5600 ⬤ harrahs.com) There are many Harrah's namesake casinos across the country. Harrah's Resort was the first casino in Atlantic City to be located off the Boardwalk, in an area virtually inaccessible to pedestrians and without a beachfront. As this was a calculated risk, they compensated by making the resort a bit classier, more all encompassing, and generally nicer. Though the **Borgata** and other citywide renovations have dwarfed the quality of Harrah's in recent years, it still remains one of the nicest and friendliest casinos in Atlantic City. It is a quieter resort, but a solid top-ranking contender nonetheless.

Located directly on the bay side of Absecon Island, Harrah's Resort has over 1,600 guest rooms and suites in several different towers: Bayview, Atrium, Marina, Harbour, and the new Waterfront Tower. Depending on availability, you may be able to choose your tower. The resort features several different levels of suites, as well as rooms with views of either the bay or the ocean.

Harrah's casino almost always seems less crowded and far less cluttered than its neighboring behemoths. The large casino floor is about 140,000 square feet and has popular slot and table games. There is also a small poker room. A general ocean/marina theme carries throughout the floor, which is easily navigable.

The **Waterfront Pool** (⊗ Must See!), generally open only to adults, is one of the nicest pool areas in Atlantic City. Completely indoors (and open year-round) with a glass-domed ceiling, the pool features private cabanas, tropical trees, and even a poolside bar. The pool and environment invoke feelings of a lush tropical oasis, more like Las Vegas.

Also, **Red Door Spa** is on property for your beautification and relaxation needs and caters to both men and women with massages, hairstyling, manicures, pedicures, and facials. Poolside massages (at the Waterfront Pool) are available.

BORGATA HOTEL CASINO & SPA ⊗ Must See!
(1 Borgata Wy. ☎ 609.317.1000 ● theborgata.com) Reinventing Atlantic City, the Borgata Hotel Casino & Spa has breathed new life into a resort destination that almost seemed hopeless. The newest casino in 13 years (it opened to the public in the summer of 2003), the Borgata is a contemporary masterpiece.

Atlantic City's casinos have historically catered to an older crowd; an unfortunate trait that the Borgata is determined to thwart. The Borgata shines in many ways to convince the younger, more hip, and wealthier generations to pay this seaside destination a visit. To seduce the young and hip, features include glass-blown art pieces scattered about, wide pillared archways adorning the walking paths, and some of the most comfortable furniture in the guest rooms and lounge areas.

The Borgata is the best overall resort in all of Atlantic City. It is the cleanest, nicest, most plush, and most expensive. It has the design of a complete destination; not just a gambling hub. The spa and pool, the restaurants, the entertainment, and nightlife all shine with a modern contemporary design, a class act all the way. And without beach and Boardwalk access, visitors may almost feel like they are in Las Vegas.

Borgata's regular guest accommodations are, quite simply, the best in Atlantic City. The Borgata's only tower (not counting The Water Club next door), a sleek 43-story hotel, features just over 2,000 of the most comfortable, modern rooms available. In fact, every guest feature is designed for comfort. From **The Living Room**, a resort-guest-only lounge to the walk-in showers and extra-soft bedding in the guest rooms, Borgata seeks to surpass expectations. This luxury, however, comes at a steep price – it is the most expensive and most popular hotel in the city.

Decorated in a soothing style, Borgata's classy but stuffy casino is located in one central area on the main floor of the resort. It is easy to see the size of the 125,000 square foot area from almost any vantage point. Popular slot and table games are represented here. However, this is an expensive casino with high minimum bids, and visitors shouldn't be surprised to see a $500 slot machine. The casino also features a poker room.

Beach and ocean access notwithstanding, Atlantic City has never been like Vegas when it comes to pool and spa facilities, but the Borgata's **Spa and Gardens** takes the city one step closer. The resort houses an indoor pool, a full spa, and fitness center. In the summertime, there is an outdoor terrace open for sunny relaxation.

The spa is located on the second floor of the hotel. The largest and most obvious section is the large indoor pool and outdoor patio. The pool area is not usually very crowded. The Borgata also has the classic spa services, such as massage and aromatherapy, at its **Spa at Borgata**. For haircuts and other salon services, the salon and barbershop are nearby.

TRUMP MARINA
(Huron & Brigantine ☎ 609.441.2000 🖱 trumpmarina.com)

Trump Marina was the second of Trump's three Atlantic City casinos to open, and the second Marina District resort. Located directly on the water of Absecon Channel, it was initially called Trump Castle, but the name was changed in 1997. The resort carries a nautical theme throughout with aquatic and boat-related décor. Of course, the inherent Trumpness is all there, if not a bit dated: the chandeliers, the gold-paneled everything, the shiny decorations. Those familiar with the Donald's style will feel right at home here.

Above the central atrium is a large skylight that brings brightness into the resort that makes it appear very friendly and accommodating. Its clientèle is decidedly younger than most Atlantic City resorts, and (particularly in the summer) there are numerous entertainment options that cater to a 20-and-30-something crowd. The resort contains a total of about 800 rooms, making it the smallest resort in the Marina District of Atlantic City.

Perhaps to compensate for its Marina location, the large spa facility at Trump Marina is very impressive. The entire facility spans two floors and a surprising 120,000 square feet. It has both indoor and outdoor recreation and relaxation services. In addition to standard spa and massage services, there are outdoor tennis courts, a running track, and fitness equipment. There is also an outdoor pool which, like the rest of the outdoor activities, is only open during the warmer months.

Lodging

There are many, many motels and hotels scattered throughout Atlantic City and the surrounding area. Most of them are smaller, motel-style accommodations (guest room doors open to the outside). Some are very small, independently-operated establishments that can be rated "fair" to "of questionable quality." If you plan on rolling the dice and staying at one of these smaller, motel-style accommodations, expect to receive minimal frills. The major upside, however, is that the prices are usually much cheaper than their casino counterparts (which are, in many cases, right across the street).

If you can't (or don't want to) stay at a casino-resort, consider staying at one of the following off-resort hotels, which are among the best non-casino hotels in Atlantic City. Prices for these places are usually cheaper than their casino counterparts, but they can be much more peaceful, without the pressure to gamble. The hotels are rated $ = least expensive, $$ = moderate, $$$ = more expensive.

IN ATLANTIC CITY

A trip down Atlantic or Pacific Avenue will yield dozens of motels in Atlantic City. Unfortunately, visitors are hard-pressed to find quality accommodations that aren't part of a casino. Luckily, there are a few diamonds in the rough.

THE WATER CLUB ✪ Must See!
(1 Renaissance Way ☎ 800.800.8817 🖱 thewaterclubhotel.com)
The Water Club is by far the best non-casino hotel in Atlantic

City. Though it is technically attached (via an indoor walkway) to the **Borgata**, it is a complete destination and a world apart from its casino counterpart. This separation allows visitors to escape the hubbub of the nearby Borgata. The lobby is a modern masterpiece, a bit stuffy and foreboding if you're traveling casually. The adjacent **Sunroom** (a kind of lobby lounge) is an indoor tropical-themed bar, with walkways and chairs decorated with trees and foliage – basically a place to hang out and drink.

The hotel features both indoor and outdoor pools. The year-round indoor pool (on the ground floor) is much nicer, with decorative trees, lounge chairs, and drink service. The outdoor pool offers similar amenities, plus rentable cabanas.

Rooms are exquisite – contemporary in design but not as nice as the Borgata's; rooms and suites are both available. Some visitors have found the guest room walls to be thin, but otherwise this is a top-notch hotel, very expensive but high on the splurge-factor *($$$)*.

THE CHELSEA
(111 South Chelsea Ave. ☎ 800.548.3030 🖱 thechelsea-ac.com)
The Chelsea bills itself as the first non-gambling hotel to be built directly on the Boardwalk since the 1960s. It is a combined, remodeled version of two old hotels, a Howard Johnson and a Holiday Inn. Now, however, it is completely unrelated to any chain or major resort, and sits within easy walking distance to several downbeach casinos. It is a nice new touch to the Atlantic City Boardwalk and a great step in the right direction.

Two guest room "towers" are available at the Chelsea. **The Luxe**, closest to the Boardwalk, is the 20-story, 200+ room tower that faces the ocean. Many rooms have ocean views. These are more expensive and resemble a "typical" hotel room – it is the "main" hotel. The other tower, called **The Annex**, has 150-ish rooms that face either the street or the ground-floor pool (many have balconies). The Annex is called the "social" wing of the hotel, which basically means that the rooms are more cramped and less expensive. Some are available in suite configurations. This room style is actually commonplace for other hotels along the Jersey Shore, but is rare for Atlantic City. Both The Annex and The Luxe have bright, modern appointments, with a romantic, modern feel, though The Annex is less classy. An outdoor rooftop pool and a ground-floor saltwater pool are both open seasonally – the rooftop pool offers bar service.

Several restaurants and "social gathering places" are available on-site, mostly on the fifth floor: steakhouse **Chelsea Prime** and diner-style **Teplitzky's**, which is named for the owners of the original hotel on the property. *($$)*

COURTYARD BY MARRIOTT
(1212 Pacific Ave. ☎ 609.345.7070

courtyardatlanticcityhotel.com) The only Marriott in Atlantic City proper, this Courtyard is modern, clean, sharp, and inviting. A lobby bar, open nightly, integrates well with the modern lobby seating area. It has an exercise room and an adjacent hot tub, but no swimming pool. Rooms are surprisingly large and well-kept. Breakfast is served every morning in the **Courtyard Café**. While off the Boardwalk, it is only two blocks away from **Resorts** and **Trump Taj Mahal** on the north end of town.

There is not much going on immediately surrounding the hotel, so you'll have to go to a casino for more activity. *($$)*

DAYS INN ATLANTIC CITY BEACHFRONT

(Boardwalk at Morris Ave. ☎ 609.344.6101

⬡ atlanticcitydaysinn.com) The best feature of this Days Inn is its location on the Boardwalk. The rooms are small and standard, generally clean, and some have balconies overlooking the Boardwalk. The prices are expensive due to its great location near the **Tropicana**. A **Country Kitchen** restaurant is on the premises. Note: There is another Days Inn in Atlantic City, not located on the Boardwalk. If staying on the Boardwalk is a priority, make sure you book *this* Days Inn.

SHERATON ATLANTIC CITY HOTEL

(2 Miss America Way ☎ 888.227.6667

⬡ sheratonhotelatlanticcity.com) This hotel is almost strictly business. Before the recent development of quality non-casino hotels in Atlantic City, the Sheraton Atlantic City has been called Atlantic City's best non-casino hotel. It is off the Boardwalk, offering very easy access to both the **Atlantic City Convention Center** and the **Atlantic City Rail Terminal**. It is also located directly opposite **The Atlantic City Outlets**. For those attending conferences or conventions, Sheraton's location can't be beat.

Just off the lobby is a small Miss America showcase featuring replicas of dresses worn by contestants during the course of Miss America's run in Atlantic City. The exhibit makes for an interesting diversion. Of course, the hotel also has an indoor pool, a business center, and is clean, upscale, and typical Sheraton. *($$/$$$)*

THE FLAGSHIP RESORT

(60 North Main Ave. ☎ 609.343.7447 🖱 fantasearesorts.com)
The Flagship Resort is just about as north on the Boardwalk as you can get, far away from the casinos and much of what makes Atlantic City unique. It is beyond even where the Boardwalk turns west, on the northern tip of Absecon Island. In fact, Flagship is not even on the Boardwalk: a road separates it – and no ocean swimming is allowed on this section of the Boardwalk.

The Flagship is primarily a timeshare resort operated by FantaSea Resorts, but guest rooms are generally available. The hotel features, among other amenities, an indoor pool. There is an antiquated feel to the resort, with a sea theme, more reminiscent of the larger hotels elsewhere on the Jersey Shore. Prices are reasonable, but the location leaves a lot to be desired. Some rooms have balconies with great views of the surrounding ocean. *($/$$)*

ATLANTIC PALACE SUITES

(1507 Boardwalk ☎ 609.344.1200 🖱 atlanticpalacesuites.com)
Atlantic Palace towers on the Boardwalk just like the nearby casinos, so it's hard to believe that this is actually a non-casino hotel. The rooms are suite-style, and some of them are rather large, with reasonable prices, even during the peak season. Despite the larger size (they bill as "suites") the rooms are antiquated, with minimal frills and amenities. Atlantic Palace is also home to a **Bluegreen Resorts** property (🖱 *bluegreenrentals.com),*

a timeshare company, so visitors to Atlantic Palace will share some amenities (including the outdoor pool) with timeshare vacation owners. *($/$$)*

HOTELS OUTSIDE OF ATLANTIC CITY

The rule here is very simple: if you are vacationing in Atlantic City, don't stay outside of Atlantic City. While the hotels/motels along Black Horse Pike, White Horse Pike, in Absecon, or any of the nearby areas may be just fine, they are usually more than five miles from the Boardwalk. You'll find a **Hampton Inn**, a **Fairfield Inn**, a **Ramada**, and a plethora of other chains within about five–15 miles of Atlantic City. Some of these hotels may have (limited) shuttle service to the casinos, but they don't offer the convenience or oceanside ambience that hotels and motels closer to town offer.

Prices, on the other hand, can be much cheaper if you leave Atlantic City. It is not uncommon to find a room for $40 a night on a weeknight (weekend prices, particularly in the summer, remain high).

Amusement Centers

Roller coasters. Midway arcades. Redemption games. Hot dogs and cotton candy. Atlantic City's Boardwalk has a history of being jam-packed with various amusement attractions of many kinds. From thrill rides to sideshows to everything in between, Atlantic City has been host to some of the wackiest amusements on the east coast, or any coast. The Boardwalk has always been where all the action takes place – and with few exceptions, most of the amusement centers today are on the same stretch they've always been.

Today the amusement centers have been toned down a bit from their illustrious past. Thrills and excitement, however, are still around. Two of the four piers in Atlantic City are host to amusement attractions. Additionally, several smaller arcades align the Boardwalk. There are some off-property amusement attractions as well.

STEEL PIER

(Virginia Ave. & Boardwalk ☎ 609.345.4893 🌐 steelpier.com)
Steel Pier is Atlantic City's answer to the other amusement piers along the Jersey Shore. It is located directly across from the **Trump Taj Mahal** and is only accessible from the Boardwalk. Though not as extensive as the piers in Wildwood or Seaside Heights, Steel Pier is a definite must if you are traveling to Atlantic City with a group of youngsters.

Steel Pier first opened during Atlantic City's golden age; in 1898. Since then it has had several ups and downs like everything else in the city. When Donald Trump leased the land from **Resorts** to complete Trump Taj Mahal, the pier was vacant, and sometimes even used for storage. But when tourism began to rise even more, the pier found its way back to becoming an amusement center once again, focusing its attention on family entertainment.

Today, the pier has everything you'd expect. Before heading out onto it, you have your choice of many amusement park favorite foods – cotton candy, funnel cakes, corn dogs, you name it! As you enter (free admission, but pay-per-ride) you are surrounded by midway games galore. Beyond the games are the rides – Steel Pier has the standard fare – a water flume ride, Tilt-a-Whirl, Ferris wheel, bumper cars, and more. No major attractions, but plenty of small ones to satisfy your amusement needs for a few hours.

Crazy Mouse is Steel Pier's claim to a roller coaster. It's the most visible attraction from the beach and neighboring resorts. However, it's not like a typical roller coaster. Think of it as a combination of those spinning teacup-style rides and a traditional track coaster – your coaster's cart spins as you make your way across the twisty track. If you tend to get a little queasy, this ride will definitely make you wish you hadn't eaten that last corn dog.

Steel Pier is thin and long, packing all the attractions close together. There is not much room on the pier, which also makes it feel very cramped and crowded even though there may not be many people around. By the time you make it to the eastern tip, you have seen it all. For the real thrill-seekers (or willing sightseers), a quick helicopter ride at the end of the pier is a great experience. It will give you the opportunity to get a perfect view of the Atlantic City skyline and to take some great aerial photographs.

CENTRAL PIER ARCADE & SPEEDWAY

(Tennessee Ave. & Boardwalk ☎ 609.345.5219) Located on the site of the world's first successful amusement pier, the Central Pier Arcade & Speedway is in the resort-devoid section of the Boardwalk between **Bally's** and **Resorts**.

The pier is primarily a video arcade with redemption games. However, the most notable aspect of Central Pier is the large go-cart track way down at the far end of the pier.

Applegate's Pier, the world's first successful amusement pier, was completed in 1884. Though another amusement pier had been built just three years earlier, it was destroyed in a matter of months due to inadequate infrastructure. However, Applegate's Pier was more subdued and relaxing, offering visitors a quieter escape.

PLAYCADE ARCADE

(2629 Boardwalk 🖰 playcade.com) Between Boardwalk Hall and the **Tropicana** is the Playcade Arcade. As one of the largest and oldest amusement arcade centers in Atlantic City, Playcade offers diversions of various sorts. They have skill-stop slot machines, arcade and video games, redemption games, and more. The indoor facility is open year-round, sometimes until late at night. It is currently Atlantic City's longest continuously-operating non-casino video acrade.

Playcade has a wide selection of arcade games despite its smallish space. They have some new releases but mostly established classics. The redemption counter – located at the back of the establishment – has a variety of prizes for those playing redemption games.

Amusement Centers

ATLANTIC CITY MINIATURE GOLF

(1 Kennedy Plaza ☎ 609.347.1661 🖱 acminigolf.com) Within the Kennedy Plaza area is Atlantic City Miniature Golf, which occupies a very unique space. As you stroll down the Boardwalk, it will undoubtedly come as an unexpected surprise to see a mini-golf course. It does not fit in with the surrounding environment. If you're traveling as a family, then this is one of the better diversions in Atlantic City.

Located almost immediately across from Boardwalk Hall, Atlantic City Miniature Golf looks almost temporary at first; like artificial golf greens have been laid out onto the Boardwalk and could be blown away by a stiff breeze at any time. This is the beauty of it though: instead of transporting you to a pirate's cove or some other far-off place, it takes advantage of its very unique location. You are golfing on the Atlantic City Boardwalk.

As is to be expected, this is a very popular attraction, so expect to spend some time waiting, especially during the hot summer months. It is a full 18 holes of mini golf and can take a few hours out of your day. But for families or couples, this can be great fun. The course is open during the evening hours as well, and twilight golfing can be especially unique.

The course is not as challenging as other mini-golf courses; this can be a disadvantage if you're a seasoned mini-golfer. But all the basics are there: waterfalls, fountains, and crazy golf greens. But what isn't basic is the beautiful beach and massive Atlantic Ocean – right next to the course. *($)*

Atlantic City

STORYBOOK LAND

(6415 Black Horse Pike ☎ 609.646.0103 ▮ storybookland.com)

Located just outside of Atlantic City, Storybook land is a small, 20-acre theme park catering to families with young children. It is designed with classic children's stories and poems in mind, and throughout the park these stories are represented in various rides and attractions. Despite the small size, however, Storybook Land really packs a lot in. It is a very cute and worthwhile family diversion.

There is a quality about Storybook Land that makes it a very attractive place to visit – it is not large and noisy like other theme parks, but rather relaxing and extremely homey. The ride selection includes: a small roller coaster, a train ride, an old-time car driving track, and several other small and gentle rides. The property is very grassy and wooded, with plenty of places to relax. Seasonally, Storybook Land has some special events. Around Halloween and Christmas, the park is dressed up for the occasions, with special attractions (like a visit from Santa Claus in Christmas and a purposefully-not-scary hayride for Halloween).

Storybook Land has been owned and operated entirely independently since 1955. The yearly operating schedule is generous; they are only closed for about three months out of the year (January through March). During November and December, the park has late afternoon hours on weekends. Ticket prices are reasonable – less than $25, and includes unlimited rides and attractions for the day. Repeat visitors may be interested in purchasing a season pass.

Overall, Storybook Land is a very kid-friendly amusement park without a lot of the loud, flashy entertainment options found elsewhere. *($$)*

Entertainment and Sports

In addition to the venues within the main resort hotels, Atlantic City boasts several prime locations for shows, entertainment, and sporting events. Some of the placesin and around town (such as Boardwalk Hall) have historical significance as well as current uses. Unlike Las Vegas, much of Atlantic City's entertainment and sport venues are integrated with the local community, New Jersey as a whole, and, to an extent, Philadelphia. They are treated not as stand-alone theaters designed for one resident act, but rather as a venue for touring celebrities and groups.

BOARDWALK HALL ✪ Must See!

(2301 Boardwalk ☎ 609.348.7000 ☎ boardwalkhall.com) The Atlantic City Boardwalk Hall was first conceived of in 1910, and eventually manifested into a building for its grand opening on May 31, 1929. Back then it was called the Atlantic City Convention Hall, but since the opening of the newer off-Boardwalk convention center in 1997, the original is now referred to as the "Boardwalk Hall." It is located near the southern section of the Boardwalk, in between the Midtown and Downbeach resort areas. Directly on the other side of the convention center is **Kennedy Plaza**, which hosts seasonal activities such as concerts and mini-golf.

Declared a National Historic Landmark in 1987, the building underwent extensive renovations and restorations, including making better use of the space for various technological innovations that were not available during the building's initial opening. There was an additional renovation in 2001, costing about $90 million, which finally brought the hall up to par with the best venues around the country.

The building's exterior has a semi-circle shape, with a hard concrete texture. It has that "historic" look, which is much different than the surrounding resort-hotels. It has a subdued, classically elegant appeal and lays much lower than the neighboring towers. While entering from the street side is less-than-attractive (you will see various utilitarian entrances and garbage pick-up stations), the Boardwalk entrance is grand, and a real step back into the history of Atlantic City architecture.

The Atlantic City Boardwalk Hall has two different venues, which can host a variety of different kinds of events. The main hall is used for boxing, hockey, and other sports, as well as concert events or shows. It is the largest single event center in Atlantic City, which can accommodate over 13,000 people. The hall has hosted numerous indoor sporting events and, for many years, the Miss America Pageant. For a time, it even served as the home for a minor league hockey team and an indoor football team.

On occasion, neighboring casinos such as **Bally's** will take advantage of the **Adrian Phillips Ballroom**, since Bally's does not have a large venue of its own. The well-known SMG management company, headquartered in Philadelphia, manages the entire venue.

In addition, the Ultimate Fighting Championship holds occasional events here, as well as professional boxing matches, and countless concert tours. As it is the largest venue in Atlantic City, many big names are drawn to the hall. If you are interested in visiting or would like to know about a specific event, you can inquire by contacting Boardwalk Hall's box office, or online at Ticketmaster.

ATLANTIC CITY AIR SHOW

(Atlantic City Boardwalk ⏽ atlanticcityairshow.com) One of the most popular seasonal events in Atlantic City is the annual Atlantic City Air Show. The sky over the Atlantic Ocean becomes a stage for wild aerial antics, stunts, military planes, and a wide range of sky-centric performances. Down below, on the Boardwalk, over a quarter of a million people gather to watch the event annually. This is an extremely popular free event that draws more people to the Atlantic City Boardwalk than at any other time of year. It is a real crowd pleaser and lots of fun for the whole family. For specific date information, visit their Web site.

KENNEDY PLAZA

(Georgia Ave. & Boardwalk) Directly across from the Atlantic City Boardwalk Hall is Kennedy Plaza, which is, among other things, a restful showcase and stage, and an outdoor garden. The plaza fits in well with its Boardwalk Hall counterpart on the opposite side of the Boardwalk. It is partitioned from the beach with a large stone structure, complete with evenly-spaced pedestals. As with the hall itself, it feels very structurally permanent, with well-groomed and maintained stone décor. Although accessible and open free to the public year-round, it is particularly stunning during the summertime, when the flowers and plants within the garden are at their peak of color.

In the center of the plaza is a statue of a worker. The large stone plaque next to it is dedicated to people that passed away while working on Atlantic City's redevelopment since 1979. The statue was erected on April 28, 1998 and serves as a centerpiece for the plaza. Beyond the statue, against the far back of Kennedy Plaza, is a bust of John F. Kennedy himself.

Of particular note to perform on stage at Kennedy Plaza is the **Chicken Bone Beach Jazz Concert Series**. Every summer on a weekly schedule, groups sponsored by the Chicken Bone Beach Historical Foundation perform at the plaza to commemorate African-American heritage in Atlantic City. Chicken Bone Beach – the unofficially dubbed strip of beachfront south of Missouri Avenue – was where African-American families wishing to vacation in Atlantic City were restricted to between the 1900s and the 1950s.

SKATE ZONE

(501 N. Albany Ave. ☎ 609.441.1780 📱 flyersskatezone.com)
The Philadelphia Flyers Skate Zone is a chain of family-friendly, indoor ice-skating facilities owned by Comcast-Spectacor (parent company of the Philadelphia Flyers as well as other sport teams and venues). Headquartered in Philadelphia, they operate area facilities in several locations, including Voorhees, Bethlehem, Pennsauken, and Atlantic City.

The Atlantic City facility opened in 1999, and caters mostly to local interests. Several clubs and local groups make use of the indoor rink, which is open nearly year-round. Several groups use the facility on a regular basis, including youth hockey clubs, figure skating clubs, and a collection of other groups that come from the nearby area. Nonetheless, there is also almost always daily rink time (call for schedule) devoted to free skating and is open to the public.

The facility is equipped to rent skates and also has a pro shop ("**Pro Zone**"), a small arcade, a snack bar ("**Snack Zone**"), and of course, an ice rink with an audience capacity of about 300. *($$)*

GOLF COURSES

Golfing is a big deal on the Jersey Shore, and the area is peppered with golf courses with different sizes and attractions. Although no professional courses are directly within Atlantic City, a short drive inland can be fruitful for anybody wishing to enjoy a day on one of the area's courses. Pay-per-day rates for these facilities can cost around $60-$100 or more, depending on the day of the week, or what time of day you wish to golf.

BLUE HERON PINES GOLF CLUB
(550 W. Country Club Dr., Egg Harbor City 🖱 blueheronpines.com)
Blue Heron Pines Golf Club is a pay-per-game facility that offers two different 18-hole courses to choose from. Frequent golfers can also enjoy various levels of membership that allow course access on a more regular basis. On occasion, golf packages may be available with select area resorts and hotels.

TWISTED DUNE GOLF CLUB
(2101 Ocean Height Ave., Egg Harbor Township ☎ 609.653.8019 🖱 twisteddune.com) The Empire Golf Management is responsible for the daily management of several courses around the greater Atlantic City area. One of their public courses in particular, the Twisted Dune Golf Club offers 18 holes of various ratings, as well as practice and teaching facilities.

HARBOR PINES GOLF CLUB
(500 St. Andrews Dr. ☎ 609.927.0006 🖱 harborpines.com)
Harbor Pines Golf Club is a pay-per-day 18-hole golf course, which also features a collection of on-site homes in gated-community-style, called "Harbor Pine Estates." The course's

club house is particularly large and well-appointed. Of course, membership options are also available for frequent golf enthusiasts.

SEAVIEW RESORT AND SPA

(401 South New York Rd., Galloway Township 🖰 seaviewgolf.com)
For a more all-encompassing golf outing, Seaview Resort and Spa, a **Marriott** resort, is a complete resort complex that has all kinds of activities, as well as two full 18-hole golf courses. Though it particularly caters to golfers, the resort has tennis courts, indoor and outdoor pools, a business meeting space, an on-site restaurant, and a full health club.

ATLANTIC CITY COUNTRY CLUB

(🖰 harrahs.com/golf) If you wish to experience a private country club but without all the fees involved, the Atlantic City Country Club is open only to those guests staying in an area resort owned by **Harrah's Entertainment**. For more information about this golf experience, contact the Harrah's Entertainment resort you wish to stay at prior to booking.

Museums and Culture

In 2004, Atlantic City celebrated its 150th anniversary. Though the attractions and culture have changed dramatically since 1854, it is a history still alive today in many of the area's attractions, the city's structure, and commerce. Visitors will appreciate today's attractions and development all the more with an understanding of the city's past. Over time, many important historical figures have graced the beaches and Boardwalk, each leaving their mark. Many firsts, many oddities, and many corporate entities found their way to this spot on the coast. Visitors are often amazed to learn that there is much more to Atlantic City than the beach and casino-resorts. As a testament to its long and winding history, the Atlantic City of today is host to many cultural options, from museums to monuments and memorials. Some attractions are preserved relics from the past, while others are newer additions to a constantly expanding city. Cultural attractions are located both on and off the Boardwalk.

GARDEN PIER

(New Jersey Ave. & Boardwalk) Historically, Garden Pier has always been the calmest pier in Atlantic City. When it first opened to the public in 1913, it was an outdoor theater, decorated with ornate flowers and plants. If visitors were looking for an afternoon of cultural refinement and sun, basically your only option in Atlantic City would be Garden Pier.

This is also true today. As the northernmost pier, it is located almosy immediately across from **Showboat**, at the far north end of town. Despite its remote location, Garden Pier is a definite cultural highlight within the city. It is host to two distinct

Museums and Culture

buildings. The **Art Center** is to the left as you enter the pier's steel gate, and the **Historical Museum** is on the right.

ATLANTIC CITY HISTORICAL MUSEUM

(Garden Pier ☎ 609.347.5839 🖱 acmuseum.org) The Atlantic City Historical Museum features comprehensive displays highlighting important moments in Atlantic City history. The museum is a small room, but is jam-packed with artifacts and information, and it offers a great insight into Atlantic City's first 100 years. It features a permanent exhibit, called "Atlantic City, Playground of the Nation" with all kinds of memorabilia such as souvenirs, photos, clothes, and posters. Visitors can learn about the Boardwalk, the many amusement piers that have come and gone, and the political and corporate giants (such as H.J. Heinz and George Tilyou) that have graced the city. Of particular note is the wide array of Miss America-related articles and the "pickle pins" which are still available.

The museum also showcases a documentary on Atlantic City history, called *Boardwalk Ballyhoo: The Magic of Atlantic City*. Copies of the documentary can be purchased at the small gift stand at the entrance to the museum. The stand also sells historical books and unique gift items. On occasion, the museum houses temporary exhibits.

ATLANTIC CITY ART CENTER

(Garden Pier ☎ 609.347.5837) Also located on **Garden Pier**, next door to the museum, is the Atlantic City Art Center. Though not focused on historical interests like its next-door neighbor, it houses three galleries featuring a rotating schedule of art exhibits. The works on display are often-times for sale and feature a particular artist. Overall, the

Atlantic City Cultural Center on Garden Pier is a definite must-see for any first time visitor to Atlantic City. *($)*

THE NEW JERSEY KOREAN WAR MEMORIAL

(Brighton Park & Boardwalk) Almost exactly where **Bally's Park Place** meets the Boardwalk, sandwiched between **Brighton Park** and Bally's Park Place, is the New Jersey Korean War Memorial. It is accessible immediately off the Boardwalk. As you enter the small enclave, you first notice two distinct walls, one made of granite and etched with names of servicemen who died during the Korean War, and one of sand-colored stone, with reliefs of American soldiers emerging out of it. A statue in the center is of a single soldier, with his helmet off, holding onto several ID tags. In warmer weather, water cascades down from the memorial wall.

This is a totally free outdoor memorial dedicated to those who fought in the Korean War. Around 250 people attended the groundbreaking on March 14, 2000, and it opened to the public on November 13 that same year. It is a touching tribute to those who served; those who returned, and those who did not.

DANTE HALL THEATER OF THE ARTS

(14 N. Mississippi Ave. ☎ 609.344.8877 ⬢ dantehall.org) Not a stone's throw from the entertainment of the casinos on board-walk is Atlantic City's answer to classic culture. Dante Hall is – as the name suggests – a performing arts venue that has a regular calendar of predominately musical productions (check the Web site for schedules). The theater was built in 1926 and had fallen into great disrepair. Now completely renovated (in 2003), performances at Dante Hall are once again regular.

Museums and Culture

CIVIL RIGHTS GARDEN

The Civil Rights Garden is a small garden with a winding walkway, a reflecting pool, and statues that seem to burst through the ground. Each of these statues has inscriptions of important people and places in the history of Civil Rights. In the center of the garden is a large bell (similar to the Liberty Bell), which rings during special occasions.

The garden features a nice landscape of flowers and plants (particularly in the summertime). Though it feels peaceful, there is definitely a feeling of gravity as you pass through the garden's gates. A wrought iron fence encapsulates the many pedestals. Visitors guide themselves along the path, stopping at the pedestals to read the inscriptions.

RIPLEY'S BELIEVE IT OR NOT! MUSEUM
(New York Ave. & Boardwalk ☎ 609.347.2001 🖱 ripleys.com)

Wherever there is a tourist town, there seems to be a Ripley's Believe It or Not! Museum. If you are driving towards a town with billboards for mini-golf, go-carts, or roller coasters, and fudge shop after fudge shop, chances are you'll see a Ripley's. Atlantic City, Niagara Falls, Myrtle Beach, Wisconsin Dells, and many other towns have this particular attraction.

The Ripley's museum in Atlantic City is located directly on the Boardwalk by the ocean, sandwiched between two large resort-hotels. It is located between **Bally's** and **Resorts**, in a two-story high building designed to look like it has just been whacked with a colorful wrecking ball, which has been decorated to look like Earth. The exhibits inside include a replica of the Jersey Devil skeleton, as well as some classic Ripley "artifacts," such as shrunken heads, unusually talented contortionists, and people who smoke cigarettes through their eyes.

Robert Leroy Ripley was born in 1890 in Santa Rosa, California. In 1908, he sold his first comic to *LIFE* magazine. After working for the San Francisco Chronicle and Boston's *The Globe,* he decided to travel abroad. In 1918, he drew a cartoon featuring sports oddities, and one year later, drew a comic called *Believe It Or Not!* From then on, Ripley traveled the world in search of oddities to write about and publish in his comic strips. In 1929, his strips earned syndication, read by millions worldwide. Ripley would work for radio, create short films, and explore different avenues for his *Believe It or Not!* idea. In 1933, the first "Odditorium" museum opened in Chicago, followed shortly thereafter by one in San Diego and then in Dallas. In 1939, there was even an Odditorium opening in Times Square in New York City. In 1949, Robert Ripley collapsed on the set of his television show, and died shortly thereafter. The first Odditorium to open its doors in Atlantic City was in 1954 – but it closed in 1957.

Unlike many non-resort attractions, Ripley's Believe It or Not! Museum is open year-round, so even in the dead of winter you can walk through and enjoy the wonders. The entire museum tour is self-guided, and you can go through it in as little as half an hour, but you can take as long as you wish. *($$)*

DR. JONATHON PITNEY HOUSE
(57 Shore Rd., Absecon ☎ 609.569.1799 🖱 pitneyhouse.com)
Before there was a resort town, and well before there were casinos, there was lonely Absecon Island, nothing more than

a vast marshland surrounding a tiny village. Around 1820, after Dr. Jonathon Pitney graduated from medical school in New York, he made his way to the village, and set up his home there.

But Pitney had a dream. He envisioned a resort community on the island, and a "Railroad to Nowhere," which would bring visitors from nearby towns into this would-be vacation paradise. It was Dr. Pitney's direct involvement in the establishment of a railway system to this city by the Atlantic Ocean (ultimately dubbed "Atlantic City" by the railroad company), which earned him the title "The Father of Atlantic City."

Pitney's house was originally built in 1799, and another wing was built (by Pitney himself) in 1848. In 1997, the house was restored and added to the National Register of Historic Places the following year. Today it occasionally functions as both a historical site and bed and breakfast.

Visitors may tour the Dr. Jonathon Pitney House in Absecon City, or spend one or more nights in one of their especially romantic and classically appointed rooms and suites. The house and property are colonial in style, and guests are pampered with homemade breakfasts, as well as afternoon tea. The house is ideally suited for romance. Packages are available, if you are interested in a romantic getaway.

ABSECON LIGHTHOUSE ✪ Must See!
(31 S. Rhode Island Ave. ☎ 609.449.1360
🖱 abseconlighthouse.org) Nestled in between otherwise unimpressive buildings, in a mostly residential area of Atlantic City, is the tallest lighthouse in New Jersey (and the third tallest in

the United States). At 171 feet, the Absecon Lighthouse played an integral part in the development of the city and of the Jersey Shore in general. It has recently been totally renovated and today serves as a hot historical attraction. The Absecon Lighthouse is named for the island on which it is situated, and is also one of the oldest structures in Atlantic City, built well before the Boardwalk.

Dr. Jonathon Pitney, considered by many to be the Father of Atlantic City, cited numerous nautical disasters on Absecon Beach (the "Graveyard Inlet") as a reason to build a lighthouse. In 1854 the money was secured. Three years later, on January 15, 1857, the lighthouse was first lit. For years it helped sea-going vessels avoid the treachery of Absecon Beach. In 1933, the light was extinguished, and for a while the structure remained largely unused, except for some ceremonial events and mild tourism. In 1971, the lighthouse was placed on the National Register of Historic Places. After years of restorations and reorganizations, the tower itself finally opened to the public in 1999.

The Absecon Lighthouse is visible in the near distance from the northern end of the Boardwalk, particularly north of **Showboat**. Visitors may explore the gift shop, or climb the 228 steps to the viewing platform just below the lantern room. Though it is within walking distance of the Boardwalk, it is farther away than it seems, and you will probably enjoy it better by taking a short car or taxi ride, especially if you anticipate climbing to the top.

As east coasters, and New Englanders particularly, are well aware, lighthouses serve as important historical monuments. Absecon Lighthouse is among the best; but for those interested, a drive to the southern tip of New Jersey brings you to the Cape May Lighthouse, and a short drive north will bring you to the Barnegat Lighthouse. Together, these three sister lighthouses are among the most important in New Jersey. Today the Inlet Public/Private Association (IPPA) operates them. *($)*

LUCY THE ELEPHANT ✪ Must See!

(9200 Atlantic Ave. ☎ 609.823.6473 ⛊ lucytheelephant.com) For those not familiar with the eclectic history of the Jersey Shore, Lucy the Elephant is an odd thing to explain. Given the many other monstrous and goofy architectural feats of today, Lucy may not be the most impressive thing ever built. But it has a certain quality that captures the history of the area quite well.

Lucy is in the town of Margate. If only for the sake of a mild thrill, this is definitely a hyped and must-see attraction, especially if you're traveling with young people or curio connoisseurs.

So who is Lucy? She is a six-story tall elephant-shaped building (the largest "elephant" in the world). She is the quintessential roadside attraction: something totally goofy but somehow irresistible. She was initially built in 1881 as an attempt to sell real estate in the area (it has even been said that she was the area's first tourist attraction). She has been a real estate office, a summer home, a tavern, and a derelict landmark. In 1976, she was added to the National Register of Historic Places. The attraction is small, quaint, and clean.

Lucy the Elephant is an adorable attraction. She has stood the test of time, even by Atlantic City standards. The exhibits

Museums and Culture

inside Lucy highlight the history of this creation, with photographs, diagrams, and a video presentation. The whole package is very kitschy and cute. Tours are guided, although the attraction itself is small and self-contained. She was actually modeled to look like an Indian (not African) elephant, which accounts for the carriage on her back. Also, despite the fact that she has a woman's name, she has tusks and is therefore not female.

The inside of Lucy is unexpected. As the tour begins, you climb up one of her legs in a narrow, winding staircase (like that of a lighthouse), and end up in a large room, reminiscent of a turn-of-the-century courthouse. You are in Lucy's torso – there is fine oak paneling and wood flooring, and everything is clean and tidy. There are small exhibits around the outer edge of this room. In this main room, you can watch a short video on the history of Lucy; her purpose and development. Then your guide will take you up on another staircase to the very top of Lucy where there is a truly great view of the beach and of surrounding Margate.

The tour is short; don't expect it to take longer than about 20 minutes (and the video takes up most of that time). If you're looking to kill an entire day, this attraction won't do it. But if you're anywhere around, this is an honest, historical Jersey Shore landmark that is sure to please anybody. Lucy's hours fluctuate based on the season.

Aside from its size, Lucy looks obviously artificial, like a papier-mâché creation, but that's the point. The parking is limited, but don't worry – you don't need to spend much time here to really enjoy it. Just check out the small museum, take a look in the shop, and hop back in the car. The parking spaces for

Lucy would be prime for beach-goers, but parking there is not allowed, unless you buy a tour ticket. *($)*

ATLANTIC CITY AQUARIUM
(800 N. New Hampshire ☎ 609.348.2880 🖱 acaquarium.com)

The resident aquarium in Atlantic City is the Ocean Life Center. Located in the **Historic Gardner's Basin**, the center features as many as 11 large tanks filled with various species of ocean life. There is even a special tank that allows visitors to reach in and touch some of the more unusual and exotic (but safe) animals.

The tanks of the aquarium each specialize in a particular kind of ocean environment. The "Fish of the New Jersey Coast" tank contains bluegill, weakfish, kingfish, nurse sharks, and more. The "Coral Reef" tank has varieties of sea life that live in a reef environment. Other tanks include "Seahorses & Shellfish," "Tropical Beauties," "Live Moon," "Jelly Fish," and more. The center's inhabitants tend to rotate a bit due to species' availability. "Sea Sights & Sounds," "A Ships Bridge," and other permanent exhibits, as well as computer terminals loaded with marine life information, make for a well-rounded experience.

The center is rather small, but packed with things to see and do. It consists of three floors, the main floor being the main aquarium area. Most of the exhibits are visible right from the front desk, which is also a gift shop. The second floor consists mainly of interactive exhibits and sets. The top floor – the roof of the center – has an outdoor portion that offers visitors a great 365-degree view of the Basin, the Marina District, and even the distant Boardwalk skyline.

Museums and Culture

The Ocean Life Center first opened in 1999. Access by car is the most convenient. It is located near the tip of the Gardner's Basin, surrounded almost completely by water. Directly on the other side of the water are the **Trump Marina** resort and the Farley State Marina. *($$)*

BALIC WINERY

(6623 Harding Hwy. Mays Landing ☎ 609.625.2166
☷ balicwinery.com) Mays Landing has had this winery in some form since the turn of the 19th century, but wine entrepreneur Savo Balic purchased the land in 1966, renaming it the Balic Winery. At 57 acres, Balic Winery today bottles about 12,000 cases of wine per year, at six–12 bottles per case, one bottle at a time. The processing center on the property itself caters mostly to the sales of wine and wine tasting.

Tours are usually available; just ask for one. Visitors will note that Balic Winery is a functional facility and does not as much cater to tourists as do other vineyards in the area, such as **Renault Winery**. If you are interested in wine, however, and want a quick vineyard experience, Balic Winery is a good choice. For a more elaborate experience, Renault offers a more comprehensive package.

RENAULT WINERY

(72 Bremen Ave. ☎ 609.965.2111 ☷ renaultwinery.com) Located in the New Jersey Pine Barrens about 35 miles away from Atlantic City, the Renault Winery complex can be an entire vacation destination in and of itself. The property features a hotel, several restaurants, a golf course, and a vineyard complete with comprehensive tour and wine tasting. Ample space is available for weddings and conferences.

Museums
and Culture

Louis Nicholas Renault first purchased the land on which the winery sits in 1864. After having some bad luck with his vineyards in France and California, he moved his operation to Egg Harbor and proceeded to win many awards for the wine produced there. During Prohibition, the winery was sold to John D'Agostino who sold wine on a limited basis. Since then it has exchanged hands several times, until Joseph P. Milza, who currently owns and operates the entire resort, finally acquired it.

Stepping onto the main vineyard complex today feels very much like stepping into a small French vineyard. The **House of Renault** is the centerpiece of the winery, made of dark wood and surrounded by a French-influenced garden. The entry doors for the main tour are massive wooden structures. The small garden surrounding the house has a few gazebos for relaxing and gathering, and a stream of water flows throughout, with walking bridges crossing it in places. There is also a gift shop on the site as well as a place to buy Renault wine. The guided tour focuses on the wine processing, and includes history of the vineyard ("how could such a vineyard have wound up in Egg Harbor Township?"). Your tour guide will bring you into the real working rooms in the various stages of grape harvesting, fermentation, and distribution. At the end of the tour, Renault gives you the opportunity to taste some select wines.

The **Renault Gourmet Restaurant** has been touted as one of the most romantic places to eat in the Atlantic City area. Across the complex is the **Tuscany House**, a small hotel that caters to guests of the vineyard and nearby golf course. The rooms, like the rest of the resort, are reminiscent of fine

Museums and Culture

European styles. Inside is **Joseph's Restaurant**, which offers classy décor and a diverse menu.

The Vineyard Golf is a newer addition to the Renault complex. It opened in 2004 and really transforms the complex from just a hotel and vineyard to a complete vacation resort. This unique course, on some of the holes, offers a very nice view of the vast vineyard property. The course is full-size, covering about 7,000 yards on the complex. The management offers memberships as well as a tee-at-a-time option.

Guests wishing to make Renault their destination of choice have the option of several vacation packages that may include rooms, vineyard tours, gourmet dinners, and golf tee times. Call the main Renault Winery number for more information. This is definitely a must-see attraction in south Jersey. It is family-friendly for a vineyard, but there isn't much to do for those not into wine, golf, or fine dining. At one point the Renault Winery was the largest producer of wine in the United States, and it remains one of the oldest operating vineyards in the country today.

THE NOYES MUSEUM
(733 Lily Lake Rd. ☎ 609.652.8848 🖰 noyesmuseum.org)
Entrepreneurs Fred and Ethel Noyes had first hoped to open a fine art museum in south Jersey as early as 1974, when they finally provided enough money to start the pre-planning process. Unfotunately, Mrs. Noyes died in 1979 and the museum's future rested on the shoulders of the Mr. and Mrs. Fred Winslow Noyes foundation. The museum finally opened in 1983.

Museums and Culture

The Noyes Museum is directly adjacent to the **Edgar B. Forsythe National Wildlife Refuge**, in an idyllic location. It is a small museum, but full; it focuses primarily on folk art and craft (art created with practical purpose), particularly American art. The museum has a permanent collection as well as temporary exhibits. Among other displays, it has a large collection of hunting decoys as well as a selection of cottage arts, such as quilts, woodworking, and pottery. There is also a special section dedicated to art from local schools.

The museum also has a shop on the premises, where you can purchase collectible art and other exhibit-related memorabilia. There is also adequate space for corporate or private functions. Membership options are also available. *($$)*

Museums and Culture

Parks and Recreation

The Jersey Shore is host to a wide variety of outdoor activities. However, most other Shore points revolve around swimming or generic summertime activities. Atlantic City is unique in this respect – it has sports and recreational activities of all sorts, which range from the standard summertime fare to truly unique retreats and even wildlife experiences and education centers.

In addition to opportunities within the city, some significant natural and recreational activities are a short drive away from the city. State and Federal parks are abundant in New Jersey, and two of the most important ones are located just outside Atlantic City.

THE SENATOR FRANK S. FARLEY STATE MARINA

(Across from Trump Marina) One unique aspect of **Trump Marina** is the fact that it really does contain a large marina. Though Trump does not own the Farley State Marina outright, it is under the resort management and integrated directly with it. There are over 600 slips for water vessels to park. These slips can be rented in a variety of ways (for the day or for the summer, and for everything in between).

The marina is fully functional. It has electric and water services for yachts and cabin cruisers, gasoline pumps, showers, laundry, and bathroom facilities. The marina itself is owned by the New Jersey Division of Parks and Forestry, so it is not an "official" part of Trump Marina's property. It is located in a well-protected inlet with very little waves or water turbulence. The water itself is deep, and many of the Jersey Shore attractions are accessible, as the marina itself is somewhat centrally located on the Shore. **Docksider** is the Marina's official store, which sells all sorts of useful nautical thingamajigs.

BRIGHTON PARK

(North of Bally's, in front of Claridge) Separating **Claridge** from the Boardwalk is Brighton Park, a pleasant and well-maintained oasis in an area otherwise inhabited by parking lots and towering hotels. It is free to roam for guests of Claridge and anybody else with a curious eye. In the summertime, the park has a water fountain, trimmed plants, and other lush greenery, which makes for a peaceful retreat.

EDWIN B. FORSYTHE NATIONAL WILDLIFE REFUGE

(Great Creek Rd. ☎ 609.652.1665) Much of the Jersey Shore (particularly the south Shore) is uninhabitable marsh. For this reason, arriving at various Shore points, including Atlantic City, requires first traversing large land masses of flat, marshy landscape and shallow lakes. Only the very edges – just along the ocean – have been developed.

The Edwin B. Forsythe National Wildlife Refuge is about 40,000 acres representative of this type of coastal wetlands landscape. The refuge is largely inaccessible; however, there is an eight-mile expansive donation-funded vehicle "safari" within the area that gives a good impression of the land. The refuge serves mainly as a resting place for migratory birds (like portions of New York City's Gateway National Recreation Area). If you are a bird-watcher, you will feel particularly at home here. There are "patches" of the reserve located at strategic points just north of Atlantic City. The main vehicular entrance is accessible via Route 9 just north of Atlantic City (take White Horse Pike to 9 North).

The refuge is part of the New Jersey Coastal Heritage Trail. This series of parks and natural environments runs down the Jersey Shore from Sandy Hook to Cape May, and then wraps a little bit around the southern tip of the state. It is meant to be a trail for vehicles to follow down the Shore. The trail itself is not one particular "thing," but rather a collection of independent federal and state run sites that have been grouped in this manner. In other words, if you are driving down the Jersey Shore, you are exploring the Coastal Heritage Trail.

WHARTON STATE FOREST AND BATSTO VILLAGE

(4110 Nesco Rd. ☎ 609.561.0024) Wharton State Forest, approximately 20 miles away from Atlantic City, is the largest state forest in New Jersey. It is not directly on the Jersey Shore (unlike the **Edwin B. Forsythe National Wildlife Refuge**), but it is close and is a stark contrast to the Shore's natural landscape. Consisting of about 110,000 acres, Wharton covers ground in three counties: Burlington, Camden, and Atlantic. It was named after Joseph Wharton, who purchased large portions of land in the area during the late 1800s, with the intent to reap financial benefits by using the land for its agriculture and commercial assets. But Wharton passed away before any real damage to the forest was done. New Jersey purchased the land in the mid-1950s, and today the New Jersey Division of Parks and Forestry manages it. Officially, Wharton State Forest is part of the New Jersey Pinelands area.

Driving into Wharton State Forest, especially from the heavily populated Jersey Shore area, with eight or more lane highways, seems like an unusual and sudden jolt. In a matter of feet, the road changes from a massive highway to a mere two-lane country road, deeply shrouded by tall trees on either side. Signs from the Garden State Parkway and Atlantic City Expressway point to the appropriate exit to reach the forest, but don't expect it to be right around the corner.

Though most of the forest remains in its natural state, some areas within it have been developed both recreationally and commercially. There are year-round campsites scattered all around the area, particularly near Crowley Landing, Atsion, and Batsto Village. Route 542 and 206 are the two main access roads into and out of Wharton, but there are dozens of unpaved roads that take you as far into the forest as you are willing to go. There are hiking trails, natural picnic and swimming areas, and horseback riding trails.

The most significant of these is **Batsto Village,** the principal purchase of Joseph Wharton, made in 1876. Originally, however, Charles Read created Batsto Iron Works on the Batsto River in 1766. It changed hands several times since then (eventually landing on Wharton), while always maintaining its industrial iron-and-glassmaking core. Today the buildings are preserved, and visitors are free to explore the village on foot and even walk into several dozen buildings to learn about the industry of the day. Visitors will notice the buildings in Batsto Village have a historic cabin look to them. The bridge over Batsto Lake offers a great view of the small, serene lake.

If you are interested in seeing Batsto Village but want to get a taste of Wharton State Forest along the way, 542 off the Garden State Parkway (going north, take exit 50 north to 542) will take you along the southern edge of the forest – a very wooded drive – and past the water at Crowley Landing, where recreational boating is allowed. *($)*

BEL HAVEN CANOES AND KAYAKS

(1227 Route 542 ☎ 609.965.2205 🌐 belhavencanoe.com)
For the athletic nature lover, the New Jersey Pinelands area offers outdoor water canoeing and kayaking activities close to Atlantic City. Bel Haven, in the **Wharton State Forest** area, offers options such as canoeing, kayaking, and more for adventurous souls. Explore the Oswego, Mullica, Wading, or Batsto rivers either in large groups or by yourself. The rivers are generally calm, though there may be some rougher sections on occasion.

Prices are per canoe per day, but tours can run anywhere from a few hours to several days (nearby campsites are available along the various river routes). This activity requires a certain amount of athletic ability and a basic knowledge of canoeing or kayaking. However, on occasion, guided tours may be available for certain routes and seasons. Canoes are advised for two people, whereas kayaks are suitable for one. *($/$$$)*

HISTORIC GARDNER'S BASIN

(New Hampshire & Parkside Ave.) Tucked away in a small corner of Atlantic City that seems out of the way from everything else is Historic Gardner's Basin. Modeled after a New England fishing village, this small, gated area is a real unexpected and pleasant surprise. Most people traveling there are destined for either one of several privately owned Atlantic City cruises, or the family-friendly **Ocean Life Center / Atlantic City Aquarium**, but the entire area is a real treat and features several different unique opportunities (and a very nice view). And better yet, most of these attractions, even the boating excursions, can be open year-round (but call ahead during the winter months).

Gardner's Basin is located on a small peninsula immediately across from **Trump Marina**. It is near the northern end of the Boardwalk (after it wraps around Absecon Island, north of **Showboat**).

Enter the area by car or taxi via New Hampshire Avenue. The basin, named after former Atlantic City Mayor, John H. Gardner, was actually the location of the first hotels in Atlantic City. A majority of the surrounding water area is devoted to various marinas – some of which have vessels that operate public tours and charters.

The area has had its ups and downs over the years, much like the rest of Atlantic City. However, the recent renovation of Gardner's Basin allowed for the **Atlantic City Aquarium**, as well as several major renovations to the area. Now visitors can eat lunch, take a boat cruise, explore oceanography, or just walk around this unique tourist village. You may see people fishing off one of the three shores of the peninsula, or snap some photos of the Marina District. The area also offers a nice view of the bridge to Brigantine.

Gardner's Basin is a small but pretty area, scattered with fishing-village-style buildings. They look very much like small country houses that have been converted into even smaller restaurants, bars, or shops. Parking is free to visitors, so feel free to walk around a little bit.

From the main parking lot, the first establishment you'll notice is the **Back Bay Ale House** (☎ *609.449.0006*). The exterior looks small, and when you look inside, the interior is even smaller. A small bar mostly takes up the main area, but food is served both inside and on a patio outside. Also nearby is

Back Bay Ice Cream, which serves all the classic cold treats, including snacks and gelato.

The **Flying Cloud Café** (☎ *609.345.8222)* has a great water-front location, where you can enjoy a nice selection of specialty seafood dishes, including a raw bar. Some resuarants allow you to dine while you watch boats move in and out of the area.

All restaurants in the Gardner's Basin area are quick eats and very casual. The hours vary seasonally and by establishment so it's a good idea to check ahead of time by calling (although no reservations are required). Expect lots of Atlantic City locals as well as tourists. Children are very welcome here, and it can be especially rewarding after an afternoon of exploring the aquarium.

BOAT CRUISES AND CHARTERS

(New Hampshire & Parkside) If boating is your thing, there is an entire culture in New Jersey devoted to the boating industry. Marinas are abundant all down the Jersey Shore (it's a very big business) and both pleasure and commercial boaters make use of the various facilities. As a result, there is much nautical traffic in and around **Gardner's Basin**, from small boats to fishing vessels to multimillion-dollar yachts. For tourists, Gardner's Basin is the debarkation point for various boating excursions in and around Atlantic City. The tours vary from sightseeing to fishing expeditions to charters in and around the Atlantic City area. Some of these companies have walk-up opportunities, while others require a special reservation.

If you are just interested in a general tour of Atlantic City, **Atlantic City Cruising** (☎ *609.347.7600)* is your main choice.

They offer cruise options that sail at various hours of the day in the summertime, including a Harbor Tour. Wintertime cruises are available by charter.

If you want to do some fishing, you may be able to do it from the shorelines of the Gardner's Basin area, or you could check out one of the three fishing cruises. **Shore Bet Fishing** (☎ *609.345.4077)* offers half-day trips as well as nighttime fishing. Or you can book a seat on the **High Roller** *(*☎ *609.348.3474)*, a large pontoon boat. Though some of these companies may be available for private charters, **Atlantus Charters** (☎ *609.408.3564)* makes that a priority – you can even book scuba diving or other special requests with them.

EXTREME WINDSURFING
(7079 Black Horse Pike ☎ 609.641.4445
🖱 extremewindsurfing.com) Lakes Bay, located on the southern tip of Atlantic City and accessible via Black Horse Pike, is a favorite local place for water sports. As the lake is part of the larger marsh that comprises much of the Jersey Shore's coastal wetlands, it is shallow and motor-powered boats have limited access. With almost consistent wind, this is an ideal place for windsurfing or kite surfing.

Extreme Windsurfing, located right next to Lakes Bay and the **Hampton Inn,** is well equipped for both beginning and advanced windsurfers. In addition to sales and rentals of all types of equipment and accessories, it also offers lessons on the sport. If you are interested in purchasing equipment, Extreme Windsurfing allows you to try out the latest equipment before you decide to make a purchase. Windsurfers and kite surfers should be in good physical shape and have a basic knowledge of the sport. You must sign a comprehensive waiver before taking to the bay. The facilities on-site include the **Hampton Inn,** a small beach, storage, snack bar, and other amenities.

MARINE MAMMAL STRANDING CENTER

(3625 Brigantine Blvd. ☎ 609.266.0537 ⬤ mmsc.org) In 1978, the Marine Mammal Stranding Center was established to help distressed and stranded marine life in the area. Sea turtles, dolphins, whales, and other sea mammals have been assisted here, sometimes as many as 175 per year. Since opening, the center has rescued over 2,500 animals of various kinds. Originally headquartered in **Gardner's Basin**, the center is the only such facility in New Jersey, and has a federal and state permit to assist stranded mammals.

Visitors are allowed limited access to tour the facilities for a small donation. The actual rehabilitation center is off limits, but visitors can still see much of the facility, including a small museum/gallery, the **Sea Life Educational Center**. There is also an on-site gift shop featuring logo shirts, CDs, and videos. Summertime hours are generally steady, but it is strongly recommended that you call ahead, as access to the facility tends to vary greatly year-round, but especially in the winter. The center operates on volunteer services and donations. On occasion, aquatic excursions may be offered (call well in advance).

On May 26, 1978 at 10:00 a.m., as Resorts International opened its doors, the gambling era in Atlantic City was born.

Shopping

The recent major overhaul of Atlantic City entertainment centers includes the addition of several new shopping centers. Area resorts are shifting their gears towards more non-gambling establishments, and tourist retail malls so far seem to be the general direction of this trend.

CASINO SHOPPING CENTERS

Every casino in Atlantic City has several places to shop scattered around the grounds. A few casinos, however, have built entire facilities dedicated to shopping.

THE QUARTER ✪ Must See!

(At the Tropicana) On par with the latest in ever-expanding shopping and entertainment facilities, the newest major overhaul of the **Tropicana** is The Quarter. With a grand opening which occurred late fall 2004, this attraction is a major step-up for any Atlantic City resort; finally resort owners are attempting once again to draw a non-gambling crowd to Atlantic City. Other resorts are doing similar things, and even some off-Boardwalk properties are catering more to the family crowd than before.

The Quarter is a shopping, dining, and entertainment facility that features a multitude of different activities for everybody. Modeled after the resorts of Old Havana, Cuba, there are shops, restaurants, shows, nightclubs, and more. Stepping through the gateway into this heavily themed mall is reminiscent of the Forum Shops in Las Vegas, though on a smaller scale. The ceiling is domed, sky-painted with clouds, and the indoor "streets" and façades of the shops offer a sense of perpetual Cuban dusk.

Among the facilities: Tropicana has Atlantic City's first and only **IMAX Theater**. Additionally, there are several night-club and lounge areas, such as **Cuba Libre** and **Providence**. Fine dining restaurants at The Quarter include New York's **Carmine's**, **Palm Restaurant**, **P. F. Chang's**, and **Red Square**.

Also enjoy browsing the classic American Midwest style at **The Old Farmer's Almanac General Store**. **Jakes Dog House** sells luxurious and humorous items for pets. Of course, there are also clothing and jewelry stores, such as **Erwin Pearl** and **Chico's** and even **Brooks Brothers**.

THE MARKETPLACE

(At the Tropicana) Before **The Quarter**, one of **Tropicana's** greatest features was The MarketPlace, a selection of shops, restaurants, and entertainment. The Marketplace is basically a small shopping center and food court that is contained both within the Tropicana itself and outside, along the Boardwalk. With the exception of **Hooters**, this is a family-friendly area. There are all sorts of shops and eateries around The MarketPlace; there is even a bandstand in the central area, so you don't have to be in a casino or bar to listen to live music.

These are generally casual places with laidback ambience and generally inexpensive fare. Among the choices are **Corky's Ribs & BBQ**, which offers live music from time to time, **Adam Good Deli**, and **Boardwalk Favorites**.

For just drinks and lounging around, there are some nice choices. **Firewaters** has a huge selection of beer – 101 according to their Web site. It is a bar; not terribly comfortable, but if you like beer in all its manifestations, you'll be at home!

THE PIER SHOPS AT CAESARS ⊗ Must See!

(🖰 thepiershopsatcaesars.com) On the Boardwalk, directly across from **Caesars Atlantic City** and also accessible via an indoor walkway, The Pier Shops at Caesars is a brand new multi-level shopping and entertainment complex. With an opening during the summer of 2006, the complex continues the recent revolutionary trend of Atlantic City towards non-gambling entertainment. Built on the 500,000 square foot pier that was formerly home to "The Shops at Ocean One," the new pier features a host of activities, including shopping, entertainment, and even a large-scale water-and-light show (located on the far end of the pier, and called simply, "The Show"). The same group responsible for The Forum Shops at Caesars Palace has designed this new mega-center. It is an eclectic, contemporary tourist center with four floors of activities.

The Show at the end of the pier, with regular scheduled performances, is an indoor Bellagio-style fountain show with lights and synchronized music. While definitely cute and worth at least one viewing during your trip, the space limitations leave a lot to be desired. It does its best and is an entertaining visual and audio delight – some of the special effects are great. The show lasts about ten minutes, and varies depending on whether you see it during the day or at night.

The historical pier has always been an entertainment and shopping venue. Its first incarnation was as the famous

Million Dollar Pier, built in 1906. For its time, the pier was massive, and almost always crowded with entertainment, from performers such as Harry Houdini to early Miss America pageants to politicians to all kinds of exhibits. The Million Dollar Pier was destroyed by fire in 1912, and has undergone multiple resurrections since.

Today, it is filled with entertainment and dining choices, over 90 in total, including **Hugo Boss**, **Armani**, **Bebe**, **Phillips Seafood**, and **The Continental**. The pier features great views of the ocean and the skyline.

THE WATERFRONT

(At Harrah's Resort) In line with the ever-expanding resort upgrades, **Harrah's Resort** has unveiled the Waterfront, a dining and shopping area as part of the resort's multi-million dollar renovation. Without Atlantic City's beach at its doorstep, Harrah's has created a bit of an indoor entertainment center that includes a few mid-range retail shops, a **Waterfront Buffet**, and the new **Waterfront Pool**. The most impressive feature of the new Waterfront is the indoor pool, which has been designed more like a tropical oasis than a utilitarian hotel pool.

OTHER SHOPPING AREAS

Of course, there are a collection of other, non-resort malls in and around the Atlantic City area. Some will require a short drive (or taxi or Jitney ride), while others may be easily accessible from certain points on the Boardwalk. However, all of them have a wide selection of shops.

THE BOARDWALK

You don't have to walk far on the Boardwalk to find a collection of trinket and fast-food shops. This is, of course, in keeping with Boardwalk tradition. A stroll on the Boardwalk outside any Atlantic City hotel will reveal gift and souvenir shops, tee-shirt shops, beach shops, pizza shops, and any number of beach-themed establishments. These stores, when not affiliated with a casino (most aren't), are vastly less expensive than their casino counterparts. If you're looking for a bargain or cheap souvenir, head straight to the Boardwalk.

ATLANTIC CITY OUTLETS

(Near Bally's and Caesars ☎ 609.343.0081 📞 acoutlets.com)
Like shopping but hate the high price tag on your favorite name-brand items? Then outlet shopping is the answer for you!

In recent years, Atlantic City has been trying to attract a crowd that is not expressly gamblers. A good way to do this, apparenty is to create an outlet mall. Those who love to shop will really appreciate this new outdoor mall, located off the Boardwalk, directly across from **Caesars Atlantic City** and **Bally's**.

"The Walk" (as it is affectionately called) is entirely outdoors – so you'll need to have your raincoat/sweater/whatever if you want to spend any time shopping in inclement weather. All the standards are represented: Gap, J. Crew, Banana Republic, Mikasa, Guess, and many more are coming and going as the mall matures. The Walk is regularly expanding with new stores. Who knows what stores the future will bring, though for the merchants it looks bright! It also contains lots of clean public spaces, restaurants such as Subway Sandwiches and Starbucks,

Shopping   **131**

and everything you would expect from any other mid-size outlet mall. The Walk is not in an enclosed area; it is a series of buildings compacted into a small section of town.

Additionally, walking along the street from shop to shop gives visitors an abbreviated history of Miss America. Each section is dedicated to a certain decade in Miss America's history. Engraved in the sidewalk, and on nearby signs, are biographies, pictures, and other information about past Miss America winners (if you enjoy Miss America, you may want to check out the nearby **Sheraton Hotel's** Miss America showcase near the hotel lobby, which features dresses, crowns, and more).

DOWNTOWN ATLANTIC CITY

(Northern Atlantic Ave.) Atlantic Avenue is the main non-resort shopping district in Atlantic City. In particular, the strip between **Trump Taj Mahal** and the Atlantic City Expressway is home to many local shops. Grocery stores, mini malls, pawnshops, gold/jewelry dealers, and a few restaurants are packed into this small area, which don't seem to be related to the nearby resorts. This is part of the "real" Atlantic City.

As these are all independent stores, there is no single opening or closing time, though many seem to close before dark. These shops are all located within a short walk to one of several resorts, but its best to explore this area during the day, when a lot of people are present (and before the Atlantic City "nightlife" crowd takes over). It is a shopping area with local (non-tourist) flavor.

FRALINGER'S SALT WATER TAFFY

(Two locations on the Boardwalk: Tennessee Ave. & Bally's Park

Place) Mr. Bradley had no name for his unique taffy treats (a chewy mix of corn syrup and sugar), so he let his Boardwalk patrons call it whatever they wished. On one particular day in August 1883 (the story goes), he was selling his taffy as usual. But a nasty storm blew salt water all over poor Mr. Bradley's stand. After the storm passed, a young girl ordered some taffy from Mr. Bradley, which had been drenched in the ocean's salt water. "Don't you mean 'Salt Water Taffy'?" Mr. Bradley asked the girl. Mr. Fralinger – interested in opening a taffy stand of his own – was standing nearby and overheard the remark, and the name "Salt Water Taffy" was born.

Those who have enjoyed Salt Water Taffy in candy stores across the country may not know that this treat – hardly salty or watery – is an Atlantic City original. Fralinger's Salt Water Taffy popularized the treat after he opened up his own shop in 1885. Today the shops are full-fledged candy stores, but the taffy selection is extensive. Choose from many, many different flavors, mix and match your candy pieces, or buy a box with a pre-sorted mix.

Fralinger's has two locations on the Atlantic City Boardwalk today. There are also locations in nearby Ocean City and Cape May. Those visiting from afar may also order taffy online (*fralingers.com*) or by ordering them over the phone (*1.800.93.TAFFY*). Though many companies may produce Salt Water Taffy today, Fralinger's is "officially" the original.

HISTORIC SMITHVILLE ✪ Must See!

(1 New York Rd. ☎ 609.652.7777 ▪ smithvillenj.com) In 1787 there was only Smithville Inn. Built on a common stagecoach route and run by James Baremore, the inn eventually became a popular resting place for weary travelers, as not many houses or other establishments existed in the area. However, as the years went by and more area commerce arose, the need for an inn at this spot diminished, until the property finally was abandoned sometime during the turn of the 20th century. In the early 1950s, Fred and Ethel Noyes purchased the structure and restored it into a restaurant, and the seven acres surrounding the inn would eventually become known as The Towne of Historic Smithville.

Today, the seven-acre "town," a National Historic Landmark, is a re-creation of what an east coast village looked like in the 1700s. Cobblestone streets align village buildings, and a **Village Green**, complete with gazebo, a small lake, and nearly every building is packed with handcrafts and thingamajigs for sale. Many of the buildings, purchased by the Noyes, were from sites all over this part of New Jersey. Historic Smithville is a must-see for anybody and can be a particularly fun afternoon for families with children.

The collection of shops is eclectic and shopping here can be very relaxing and enjoyable. Stores include **The Candle Shoppe**, **The Christmas Shoppe**, **Cozy Fireside Treasures**, **The Jewelry Box**, **Pocket Full of Posies**, **Country Folk**, and many more, including places to eat, from a quick bite to a lavish multi-course dinner. Aside from shopping, visitors may enjoy paddle boating on the lake, a mini-train ride; a remote-controlled boat course, a carousel, and an old-time arcade. Although Historic Smithville is open year-round, some of the other attractions are only accessible during the warmer months. **The Smithville Inn**, of course, is still there. It serves as a meeting and banquet facility.

Atlantic City

Weddings here are common, but they also serve lunch, dinner, and occasionally brunch.

Historic Smithville also has a small hospitable lodging facility available. **The Colonial Inn** (*615 East Moss Mill Rd., Smithville* ☎ *609.748.8999* ☏ *colonialinnsmithville.com)* is a bed and break-fast-style establishment located directly on the grounds. It is open year-round and features eight rooms, some of which overlook the lake. The rooms are decorated to reflect the period. Rates include private bathrooms and standard hotel amenities. However, though Historic Smithville is very family-friendly, small children are not encouraged to stay at The Colonial Inn.

Throughout the year, Historic Smithville redecorates itself with holiday themes. Throughout August and September, it is host to special events, such as concerts and sidewalk sales. One of the largest events is Oktoberfest, where arts and crafts abound. During this time, there is also a "Haunted Train Ride" on weekends. For the holidays, there is a "Christmas Train Ride" and Santa Claus himself may make a personal appearance.

Historic Smithville has enough to see and do to occupy an entire day, particularly during the summertime. Its small size and themed nature are second only to its impeccable charm. Near a city with big lights and flashy façades, the quaint and beautiful Smithville is an absolute breath of fresh air, and a must-see.

The fronts of most Atlantic City resorts face the ocean, so many visitors will enter through the back upon arrival.

Clubs and Nightlife

Atlantic City is an up-all-night kind of place. Like Las Vegas, Atlantic City is famous for its after-hours entertainment opportunities. While some major resort hotels offer generally safe, upscale clubbing experiences, the city itself has numerous other ways to kill time before the sun rises.

Atlantic City's nightlife is strictly for adults! Even the resorts' clubs and bars are meant for those over 21 (sometimes over 18). Be warned that children should not venture from the resorts during the nighttime hours. Because of the vast dichotomy between resortland and cityland, mere steps away from the casino's entrance could bring any unsuspecting wanderer into an area that he or she would prefer not to enter. Atlantic City streets off the resort properties are incredibly diverse. You may, at one moment, find yourself under the glitzy umbrella of a resort, and in the next moment on a deserted city street. So it is important to keep your wits about you.

That being said, if you're up to experiencing Atlantic City's nightlife, this section describes some of the wide range of entertainment and activities available – besides gambling of course – during the nighttime hours. Atlantic City nights begin at approximately 8:00–9:00 p.m., and facilities will close between about 2:00–3:00 a.m. (except for casinos, of course, which never close).

CASINOS

Every casino in Atlantic City, whether it is on the Boardwalk or in the Marina District, is open 24 hours a day, seven days a week. Casino gambling is by far the #1 nighttime entertainment option in Atlantic City, and very likely on the entire Jersey Shore. Few other venues across the country have such a wide operating schedule, and will be crowded even in the wee hours of the morning.

A gaming day in Atlantic City starts at 6:00 a.m. and runs until 5:59 a.m. the following morning. No matter what time of year you intend on visiting Atlantic City, and no matter which resort you visit and what time of day you go, there will always, *always* be activity on the casino floor.

But which casino is right for you? That is entirely your choice. Many people gamble only in the resort in which they are staying, whereas others casino-hop across the Boardwalk. Many people are devoted to one single players' club, whereas others have thick wallets with club cards from each of the resorts. One of the best features of Atlantic City, of course, is the freedom to move between resorts with ease.

RESORT BARS AND LOUNGES

Every casino resort in Atlantic City has at least one late-night bar; most have at least three or four. If you're in a resort, you're never more than a few steps from at least one place to relax and drink. Sometimes they are swanky, sometimes casual, but they are almost always open late, and almost always busy. For more information on a particular bar or lounge with a resort, see the resorts' section elsewhere in this book.

RESORT CLUBS

A few casino resorts feature an on-site nightclub. These are generally glossy, inoffensive places that can be enjoyed by young and old alike. **Casbah** in **Trump Taj Mahal** and **Mixx** in **Borgata** are among the best, but **The Quarter** at **Tropicana** and **The Pier Shops at Caesars** each have places to keep the night young. See the resorts' listing elsewhere in this book for more information.

CLUBS AT THE QUARTER

(At Tropicana) During weekend nights (past 11:00 p.m.), **Tropicana's** Quarter becomes a real club-goers' paradise. Many of the dining establishments – quiet by day – convert into nightclubs, and the younger local New Jersey crowds pack into the streets of "Old Havana" as tightly as they would during the busiest weekends at Seaside Heights. The result: a loud crowd of crazy teens and 20-something adults too young to gamble. Love it or hate it, this influx of young people has made Tropicana one of the must-go local places for a much younger crowd than is typical in Atlantic City.

40/40 CLUB

(2120 Atlantic Ave. ☎ 609.449.4040 🌐 the4040club.com) Jay Z.'s chain of bars and clubs has a home at the **Atlantic City Outlets**. This sports bar and lounge is designed to be a hip, posh place to sit and relax. The modern interior look has the feel of a contemporary casino restaurant, if a bit more claustrophobic. A wide range of drinks are available, as well as a full comfort food menu (burgers and the like). They can also host a variety of private parties. *($)*

CASBAH

(At Trump Taj Mahal 🌐 casbahclub.com) Arguably the best (or at least the most popular) club in Atlantic City, Casbah at **Trump**

Taj Mahal is very popular, especially during the summer weekends. In this mega dance club that is hyped on billboards all across Trump Taj and the rest of Atlantic City, you can dance the night away with a huge assortment of young travelers, many of whom seem to have never been to a dance club before. For those who like large and sweaty dance floors with flashing lights and pretty dancers, Casbah is a great place to be. The drinks are expensive, and the **Casbah Café** nearby serves all kind of munchies. This is a very popular club with predominantly weekend hours and long lines. *($$)*

MIXX

(At Borgata) Mixx is located in a far corner of the **Borgata's** main casino floor. It consists of two floors, two different bar areas, and several separate, private rooms. As the name suggests; it is a "mix" of personalities, both in purpose and practice. By day, it's a multi-national restaurant and bar, with a very wide selection of food and drink (particularly wine, though rum and sake are also prevalent) choices. The food is a combination of Asian and Latin cuisine.

By night, Mixx becomes one mega dance club; perhaps the biggest in all of Atlantic City. Like **Casbah** in **Taj Mahal**, the Mixx nightclub has the ambiance of Webster Hall in New York City, or even Pleasure Island at Walt Disney World. It is one of the biggest non-gambling attractions at the Borgata. So for those young (or young at heart) visitors who want to break their eardrums in one of the hippest social gatherings in an Atlantic City resort, and it's a busy weekend, definitely check out Mixx, either by day or by night. *($/$$)*

Select Restaurants

Aside from the restaurants located within the resorts themselves, Atlantic City boasts a wide range of dining options, from casual to fine dining and everything in between. This section details a few of the more popular restaurants, both in an out of the resorts, around the city. As is to be expected, Atlantic City restaurants tend to open and close, and change names or cuisines at the drop of a hat. Following is a list of select restaurants in the area. It is highly recommended that you contact any of these establishments to confirm availability. Prices are indicated as follows: "$$$" = Expensive (More than $20 per entrée), "$$" = Moderate ($10-$20 per entrée), "$" = Inexpensive ($10 or less per entrée).

CASINO RESTAURANTS

Of course, not all the casino restaurants are described here; each casino-resort will probably have a deli-style restaurant, a quick-service spot, a steakhouse, a buffet, and various other cookie-cutter places that seem to blend into the woodwork of every casino. Provided below is a sampling of some of the better casino restaurants in Atlantic City, but feel free to explore your resort (or your neighboring resorts) for a restaurant more suited to your taste.

THE OAKS STEAKHOUSE

(At Hilton Atlantic City ☎ 888.AC.HILTON) When it comes to Atlantic City steakhouses, The Oaks at the Hilton is one of the best. Their aged steaks range from New York Strip to Porterhouse. The fish selections – particularly shellfish (and lobster) – are favorite menu choices. Next to the steakhouse is the **Oaks Bar**, which serves more casual food in a more relaxed setting. *($$$)*

THE PALM RESTAURANT
(At Tropicana, The Quarter ☎ 609.344.7256 🖱 thepalm.com)
The first Palm Restaurant opened in New York City in 1926. Since then, it has expanded into a chain of steak-and-seafood restaurants from across the country. It has become widely known as an "it" place to dine, though the expansion has somewhat diminished the restaurant's former charm. Food at The Palm revolves around its "surf and turf" staples, lobster and steak, which are both available in a variety of preparations. It provides an overpriced but satisfying meal. *($$$)*

CUBA LIBRE
(At Tropicana, The Quarter ☎ 609.348.6700
🖱 **cubalibrerestaurant.com)** Presumably named after the drink "Cuba Libre," this restaurant's menu serves food that fits in well with the Old Havana surroundings of Tropicana's **The Quarter**. It's casual, but it can be loud, especially on busy weekends. Cuban food dominates the menu, from chicken to steak to chorizo sausage. On weekends, the restaurant hosts what it calls a "floorshow," which is basically the transformation of the restaurant into a show floor. Of special note is the restaurant's extensive rum bar. *($$/$$$)*

RAINFOREST CAFÉ
(At Trump Plaza ☎ 609.345.5757 🖱 rainforestcafe.com) A densely "wooded" themed restaurant, complete with trees, waterfalls, exotic creatures, and even a timed tropical rainstorm,

Rainforest Café is a popular choice for families traveling with children. The food is expensive but the theme, right down to the animatronic animals, is worth it for fans of the genre. The Boardwalk entrance is temple-like. *($$)*

THE CONTINENTAL

(At The Pier Shops at Caesars ☎ 609.674.8300
🖱 continentalac.com) This is indeed an eclectic restaurant, and the most outstanding choice at **The Pier Shops**. Ambience is a mix of modern and classic, with fireplaces surrounded by tables mixed with oddly futuristic decorations. Food is a mix of everything. Dinner choices include Kobe Beef "sliders" (small hamburgers), king crab dumplings, Mexican pizza, and Thai chicken (truly a "continental" selection). Unfortunately, dining here can get expensive, so be prepared to spend. *($$$+)*

HARD ROCK CAFÉ

(At Trump Taj Mahal 🖱 hardrockcafe.com) Trump Taj Mahal is home to Atlantic City's Hard Rock Café. In the same theme-restaurant vein as the **Rainforest Café** at **Trump Plaza**, here you can dine among famous pieces of rock memorabilia. The menu is about the same as other Hard Rock Cafés in the 170+ restaurant chain, but it is a lot of fun. Hard Rock Café is located directly on the Boardwalk, so if it's warm you can choose their outdoor eating area. *($$)*

HOUSE OF BLUES ✪ Must See!

(At Showboat 🖱 hob.com) One of the biggest draws to **Showboat** is their House of Blues, which is more than just a restaurant. The Boardwalk portion of the resort is almost entirely devoted to this popular entertainment venue. In fact, the HOB at Showboat is among the largest in the chain. A complete entertainment venue, the House of Blues includes a show venue, a small casino, the **House of Blues Restaurant**, and even some gift-shopping options. It is a definite plus for the otherwise barren northern end of the Boardwalk. Tickets for shows may be inquired about by contacting **Harrah's**. *($$)*

SPECCHIO

(At the Borgata) The upscale Specchio has the rare Atlantic City honor of being a *AAA Four Diamond* restaurant award winner. As the only restaurant to hold this title, it offers very contemporary Italian cuisine, a high price tag, and consistently busy clientèle. Chef Luke Palladino has created an eclectic Italian menu that includes, soups, pastas, seafood (including lobster), and steaks. *($$$)*

THE VIRGINIA CITY BUFFET

(At Bally's Wild Wild West Casino) The Virginia City Buffet is one of the best buffets in Atlantic City. Designed to look like a country home's porch, there are several "stations" that mimic a mini-mall of food. From **John Wang's Asian Cuisine** to the **Remember the Alamode** dessert station, the tongue-in-cheek humor of Bally's is carried throughout. You can even get a full steak cooked to order. On busy weekends, expect to make a reservation up to several hours in advance. The buffet itself is expensive. *($$)*

FRENCH QUARTER BUFFET ✪ Must See!

(At Showboat) Along with the Virginia City Buffet, French Quarter tops the list as being one of the best buffets in town.

Decorated in a southern New Orleans-style, the French Quarter serves up the standard meat-and-potatoes-style fare in a bright, festive environment. Expect to wait up to several hours for a seat during the busy dinner rushes. *($$)*

OTHER RESTAURANTS

Not all good restaurants are in the casinos; in fact, much of Atlantic City's culinary possibilities come from the independent establishments located all around town.

ANGELO'S FAIRMOUNT TAVERN

(2300 Fairmont Ave. ☎ 609.344.2439
🖱 **angelosfairmounttavern.com)** This classic Italian restaurant, which opened in 1935, features typical Italian cuisine in a casual dining setting. Angelo's also offers a banquet hall suitable for weddings or other special occasions. *($$)*

ATLANTIC CITY BAR & GRILL

(1219 Pacific Ave. ☎ 609.348.8080 🖱 acbarandgrill.com) The Atlantic City Bar & Grill began as a pizzeria in the 1980s. Today, this casual and popular restaurant serves up a mix of greasy spoon foods and finer seafood. *($$)*

RUTH'S CHRIS STEAKHOUSE

(2020 Atlantic Ave. ☎ 609.344.5833
🖱 **ruthschris-atlanticcity.com)** Part of a chain of upscale steakhouses, the Ruth's Chris Steakhouse is located within the **Atlantic City Outlets**. Their major menu items are steak dishes with the standard wine and steakhouse ambience. *($$)*

DOCK'S OYSTER HOUSE ✪ Must See!

(2405 Atlantic Ave. ☎ 609.345.0092 🖱 docksoysterhouse.com)
Having opened in 1897, Dock's Oyster House is an Atlantic City institution that features seafood in a friendly but fine dining environment. *($$)*

FLYING CLOUD CAFÉ

(800 N. New Hampshire Ave. ☎ 609.345.8222
🖱 **atlanticcityflyingcloud.com)** Very inexpensive, very casual, and very unique, this dockside greasy spoon offers bar and comfort foods (wings, chicken tenders, oysters, etc.). Located in **Gardner's Basin**, Flying Cloud has a local feel and features an outdoor deck and occasional live music. (Seasonal) *($)*

IRISH PUB & INN

(164 St. James Place ☎ 609.344.9063 🖱 theirishpub.com) This extremely casual bar and restaurant (which also has a branch in Philadelphia) features inexpensive food, Irish drinks, and snacks. There is also a tiny inn (room accommodations) but the main draw is the bar itself. Unfortunately, the location is rather inconveniently out of the way from most Atlantic City resorts, stuck between Uptown and Midtown. *($)*

KNIFE & FORK INN

(Atlantic & Pacific Ave. ☎ 609.344.1133 🖱 knifeandforkinn.com)
Originally built in 1912 as a secret club during Prohibition, the upscale, casual Knife & Fork Inn is a famous local establishment serving seafood and steak. The recently renovated dining rooms reflect the classic Prohibition-era styles, and the wine list is extensive. *($$$)*

OLD HOMESTEAD

(At the Borgata 🛗 theborgata.com) As with the rest of **Borgata**, the Old Homestead Steakhouse is simply the best steakhouse in Atlantic City. The prices are steep at this upscale establishment, but the selections are wide and the classic Borgata service is top-notch. If steak is your thing, and Atlantic City is your place, then Old Homestead will be quite a hard cut to follow, indeed. *($$$)*

TUN TAVERN

(2 Ocean Wy. ☎ 609.347.7800 🛗 tuntavern.com) Part of the **Sheraton Hotel** building, Tun Tavern is an upscale casual establishment that serves steak and seafood. It is particularly noteworthy for its on-property brewery. *($$$)*

WHITE HOUSE SUB SHOP ✪ Must See!

(2301 Arctic Ave. ☎ 609.345.8599) This landmark casual restaurant, perhaps the most famous restaurant in Atlantic City, has been visited by the likes of such celebrities as Frank Sinatra. Though a bit of a dive, the large submarine sandwiches (and particularly the bread) are regularly praised as being the best in New Jersey, and perhaps even in the Northeast. *($)*

WONDER BAR

(3701 Sunset Ave. ☎ 609.345.8599 🛗 wonderbarac.com) Featuring seafood and sandwiches, this fine dining establishment is located on the water, with an open patio during the warm months. The "Sunset Room" offers nice views of a waterway thoroughfare. *($$/$$$)*

The White House Sub Shop has been an Atlantic City favorite since the 1960s.

HISTORIC ATLANTIC CITY

Crowded Boardwalk c. 1911

Heinz Pier Entrance c. 1906

© Detroit Publishing Company

Hotels along the Boardwalk c. 1905

© Detroit Publishing Company

Looping the loop in Atlantic City c. 1901

Million Dollar Pier c. 1915, now The Pier Shops

On the Beach c. 1901

Rolling Chairs and Steel Pier c. 1900

Steeplechase Pier c. 1905

The Dennis Hotel c. 1905, now Part of Bally's

Tropicana's 2,000 guest rooms make it one of the largest hotels in Atlantic City.

Recommendations

There are many other sources to find Atlantic City information, and other places to stay during your trip. The following sources will provide additional information to help you better plan your next Atlantic City (or Jersey Shore) vacation.

TOP RESORTS

The following resorts listed below are, according to the author, must-visit landmarks on your itinerary on a trip to Atlantic City.

THE BORGATA

This is the newest resort in Atlantic City, and also one of the best casino resorts outside of Las Vegas. It is classy and expensive, with a wide array of entertainment and dining choices. Its location in the Marina District is a bit of a deterrent, but it's a place that any visitor to Atlantic City should behold.

TRUMP TAJ MAHAL

While I'll be the first to admit that Donald Trump's ideas about style aren't univrsally appealing, this is one place where all the pieces seem to fit together. Trump Taj is a large and splendid resort, with many on-site amenities and a gargantuan gaming floor.

TROPICANA

Tropicana isn't particularly classy, but its themed gaming areas, impressive shopping, wide variety of eating and drinking options, and a nice spa make it an extremely popular "younger-crowd" resort. I enjoy the ambience because it reminds me of the friendlier themed casinos along the Las Vegas strip.

TOP ATTRACTIONS

If gambling is not the reason for your visit here – even if it is – don't miss out on checking out the following attractions.

THE QUARTER

Tropicana's Havana-themed shopping and dining center mimics that of the best Las Vegas themed malls. While much smaller, it is packed with kitschy (and nicer) shops, a wide range of dining, a comedy club, a movie theater, several nightclubs, and a lot of young New Jersey club-goers on the weekends.

THE PIER SHOPS AT CAESARS

The newest (and by far the most contemporary) new pier attraction is filled with shopping and dining choices. While a bit on the expensive side, the pier offers a more upscale experience, and more mature crowds than **The Quarter**.

THE POOLS OF BALLY'S AND HARRAH'S

Atlantic City's climate and easy ocean access make world-class pool facilities unlikely, but as Atlantic City spas and pools go, Bally's and Harrah's have the best. The facilities include a wide range of fitness equipment, large pools, and several hot tubs, and even food and drink service. They are not world class, but they are the best in the city.

Recommend

LUCY THE ELEPHANT

A few miles south of Atlantic City, Lucy sticks out like a sore thumb. Visitors can have guided tours of the elephant-shaped building to learn about its history. Children especially, will be pleased. There isn't much to see, but the history is very interesting.

ABSECON LIGHTHOUSE

Like Lucy the Elephant, there isn't much to see or do at the lighthouse, but its historical interest alone is worth the trek to the top.

TRAVEL SCENARIOS

Following are vacation possibilities under various circumstances. Atlantic City vacations are tremendously flexible and hassle-free. Eat when you want, explore where you want, do what you want. These scenarios keep your options open and give you the freedom to allow your vacation to unfold however you want.

ONE-DAY GETAWAY

(**Vacation Time:** *1 Day* **Best Time to Go:** *Any time, any day*)
Atlantic City is ultra-accessible, particularly for individuals without access to a car and in a major urban area. If you fit this description, you're in luck, as your vacation can be extremely inexpensive.

Either drive, or from a major metropolitan area (such as Washington, D.C., New York City, or Philadelphia), board a casino bus service to your favorite Atlantic City resort. When you arrive, spend the day roaming the resort. Check out the restaurants, the health club, the shopping, and even the beach if it is nearby and weather permitting. Stroll the Boardwalk and take in the fresh ocean air. When you're ready to return, simply board the bus (or drive) from the resort and make your way back home.

Recommendations: The best resorts for strolling arbitrarily and enjoying the beach include: **Tropicana**, **Trump Taj Mahal**, and **Bally's Atlantic City**. Many times, however, people will want to catch a show in one of the many venues in Atlantic City. If you are interested in the entertainment, check the resort's entertainment schedules in advance, as you may not be able to buy tickets at the box office.

ON THE CHEAP

(Vacation Time: *2 Days* **Best Time to Go:** *Winter weekday***)**
The cheapest time to visit Atlantic City is Tuesday–Thursday in the winter, when prices for an on-Boardwalk resort can plummet to around $50 if you shop around. However, if you must stay in the summer or on the weekend, consider an off-resort hotel (you may need to rent a car if you don't already own one).

Plan your travel so that you arrive mid-afternoon, and are able to check into your hotel at around 4:00 p.m. Once you're situated, its time to enjoy the resort. Start off by eating an early dinner at a moderately priced restaurant. Then enjoy the evening strolling the resort and the Boardwalk. If you're near **The Walk**, Atlantic City's outlet mall, you may be able to get some shopping in before the stores close. Also, since you have an entire night, you may wish to consider exploring other nearby resorts as well; so don't feel confined to the one

Recommend

in which you are staying. In the later hours, night owls may be able to enjoy one of several night clubs, either on-property or off. Enjoy a late-night drink before heading off to sleep.

If you're an early riser, spend the morning swimming, if your resort has a pool. Then enjoy a breakfast buffet or a quick sit-down meal. Mid-morning, check yourself out of the hotel. You are now free to explore. The Boardwalk has many shops and attractions, and a beach. But don't run around too much; this is a vacation, after all! Have a late lunch and head home in the early to late afternoon.

Recommendations: The best activities for a cheap vacation are those which incur little or no cover charge. Shopping without buying is free, so take all the time at **The Walk, The Quarter**, **The Pier Shops**, or other shopping venues that suit your taste. At night, **Trump Taj Mahal's Casbah** club is sometimes cover-charge free. If youo want to splurge on a taxi ride), then head over to **Mixx** at the **Borgata**, which some-times has no cover charge. Buffets are expensive (frequently over $20 a person); so if you can, try cheaper counter service or the various fast food options available in each resort.

WEEKEND WITH THE FAMILY
(**Vacation Time:** *2 Days* **Best Time to Go:** *Summertime*)
Important Note: As stated before, family vacations can be enjoyable in Atlantic City. However, the primary audience is adults. Therefore, children should be supervised at all times, and you must be aware that Atlantic City primarily attracts gamblers. Families with children of any age should avoid off-Boardwalk property at night. Use good judgment in all cases.

That being said, a three-day, two-night vacation with children gives you the opportunity to go beyond the Boardwalk and explore the rest of Atlantic City. You will need access to a car because (1) access off-Boardwalk requires driving and (2) casino bus services require passengers to be 21 or over to receive the casino discount. Additionally, there are some very specific, not-to-be-missed family attractions, which are several miles off the Boardwalk.

With a family, a summertime vacation is a must. Plan to stay at either **Tropicana** or **Trump Taj Mahal**, which are the most kid-friendly resorts in Atlantic City. While both offer coveted beach access, Tropicana has the magnificent new **Quarter** which features an **IMAX** movie theater and numerous unique shopping venues. Trump Taj Mahal is the closest resort to **Steel Pier**, Atlantic City's amusement pier.

Arrive early in the afternoon to take advantage of daylight. Almost certainly the kids will want to explore Steel Pier first, so make that a priority on day one. The late hours of the pier mean that much time can be spent here; sometimes it is open until midnight. If you need a break from the rides, **Ripley's Believe It or Not! Museum** is nearby, and can be a pleaser for teens (younger children may find some of the exhibits scary).

For dinner, take the kids to a resort buffet (*note*: unfortunately, some buffets require patrons to be 21, such as the **Virginia City Buffet**). They are expensive but casual, and noisy kids running around may not be as much of a problem. At night, settle the kids in (if they are old enough) and have a quiet, romantic dinner or drink with your significant other.

On the morning of day two, take a swim if your resort has a pool, but don't get too tired because Jersey Shore beach is a great place to spend the hottest afternoons. Breakfast can be had at your resort's 24-hour restaurant, but if you're still full from last night, you could get away with just that extra piece of fruit that you didn't eat from last night's buffet.

If the family is interested, **Central Pier** (just south of Steel Pier) is a smaller amusement pier, which features a nice go-cart track and some arcade games. There are several other major arcades on the Boardwalk that offer a wider selection of games but without the go-cart track. These attractions are best suited for older children, mostly teens.

Storybook Land is a classic South Jersey Shore destination for very young children and their families. Definitely add this to your roster and plan at least half a day for the experience. However, for kids of any age, **Lucy the Elephant** in Margate is a must. A short drive south, this attraction is one of the best in the Atlantic City area. It is small and quaint and won't use up much time (the tour through the six-story pachyderm is rarely longer than 30 minutes).

If there is time, and it is hot enough, an hour or two on the Jersey Shore beach is tough to beat! Stake out a nice spot near your resort, lay down a towel, put on your sunscreen, and get comfortable. The beach by Atlantic City is generally less crowded than the surrounding Jersey Shore beaches, such as Margate or Seaside.

In the late afternoon, head back to the Boardwalk and check out Tropicana's The Quarter. The IMAX Theater here shows all kinds of movies, based on the current market. With the kids

Recommend

at the movies, parents can enjoy the various clubs, comedy, or dining offered at Tropicana. Spending the evening here is the best way to wrap up day two.

Sleep in on the morning of day three. You probably don't need to check out of your room until 11:00 a.m., so take advantage. After a nice breakfast, head over to **The Walk**, Atlantic City's outlet center. In addition to the many dozens of clothing bargains, there is a range of kid-friendly stores and eating possibilities. Plus, it gives you a chance to stretch your legs before the trip home.

BEACH AND BACKWOODS FUN

(Vacation Time: *2–3 Days* **Best Time to Go:** *Summertime***)**
Atlantic City's close proximity to both beach and forest make it an ideal spot for people who like the outdoors, but don't want to leave the comforts of home far behind. To experience the best of outdoor activities, plan a summertime vacation.

Arrive in the early afternoon of day one. Before checking into your hotel (you can opt for either an off-Boardwalk or on-Boardwalk resort, whichever you prefer), grab your beach towel and chair, and enjoy the hot summer sun! Jersey Shore water is surprisingly warm for a north Atlantic state.

Depending on how much you intend to do, you may decide to spend either one or two nights in the area. Relaxing on the beach is one thing, but the next day, you will enjoy the thick wooded nature of New Jersey's largest state forest: Wharton.

On day two, load up your car and drive to nearby **Wharton**

State Forest. **Batsto Village** serves as the central information area for activities in the forest, so if you're not sure what to do, head there first. Otherwise, you can hike, kayak (or canoe), horseback ride, or even camp if you have the time. The forest is large and in some places can get rather desolate.

On day three, or later on day two (depending on your schedule), jump from forested to coastal wetlands by visiting the **Edwin B. Forsythe National Wildlife Refuge**. Though mostly for bird-watching, the refuge provides a great long-distance view of the Atlantic City skyline, and an idea of what Absecon Island would look like undeveloped. The eight-plus-mile driving "safari" gives you some great panoramic views.

Recommendations: Even though summertime offers more activities, Batsto Village in Wharton State Forest is open year-round. There are many campgrounds, trails, and other outdoor activities throughout the forest and the rest of the Pine Barrens. The beach in Atlantic City is almost always less crowded than other places along the Jersey Shore. If you prefer more beach activity, consider going a few miles south on Absecon Island, to Margate or Longport (beach access sometimes incurs a fee in these neighboring communities, unlike Atlantic City, where access is always free). For daredevils, Lakes Bay offers some water sports. **Extreme Windsurfing** provides rental equipment and some training.

ROMANTIC RETREAT

(**Vacation Time:** *3 Days* **Best Time to Go:** *Crisp, chilly winter eves, when the crowds are sparse and the luxury suites are discounted*) Atlantic City is a very popular romantic destination. Spectacular ocean views, romantic restaurants, and lavish suites of every size and description make it a couple's paradise. Though most newlyweds may prefer a more exotic destination, honeymoons and wedding anniversaries are not uncommon here.

Since romantic getaways require a romantic room, a suite in one of the resorts is a must. Suites are abundant, but be warned: on weekends and holidays, suites are frequently reserved for high-profile gamblers. Therefore, you may either need to book well in advance, or consider booking on a weekday. Jacuzzi suites are popular; they are typically a regular-sized room with a Jacuzzi and shower instead of a bathtub. The highest-priced suites, with sizes sometimes exceeding 1,000 square feet, start at around $500 per night. Oftentimes, suites might not even be available unless you are a gambler.

Recommendations: The nicest resort in Atlantic City is the **Borgata**. It is located off the Boardwalk, but if you visit in wintertime and don't expect to do much resort-hopping, this setback might not matter. Pretty much every resort in Atlantic City has at least one romantic restaurant and bar. For shopping, **Historic Smithville** is a peaceful place, with plenty of romantic spots, and even paddleboats on the small lake.

WEB SITES

There are some great Internet resources on Atlantic City. When planning your trip, these Web sites provide additional information – in some cases, it may even be possible to purchase tickets or make reservations online. These Web sites are, of course, in addition to the ones that are listed with the individual attractions in this book. *Important:* this information is provided merely as a general guide; these sources are endorsed by the author or publisher of this book. *Use these outside sources at your own risk.*

ATLANTIC CITY.COM

(🖱 atlanticcity.com) This is one of many sites that allows visitors to book Atlantic City hotel rooms online. It also has special offers and rate information for both casino resorts and non-casino hotels.

ATLANTIC CITY CONVENTION & VISITOR'S AUTHORITY

(🖱 atlanticcitynj.com) This is the official Web site for the Atlantic City Convention & Visitor's Authority. It provides information on many of the resorts and attractions.

CITY ATLANTIC

(🖱 cityatlantic.com) This Web site provides reviews of resorts and attractions, as well as special events and entertainment schedules.

CITY OF ATLANTIC CITY

(🖱 cityofatlanticcity.org) This is the government Web site for Atlantic City, featuring information about the city on a more political level.

GREATER ATLANTIC CITY TOURISM COUNCIL

(🖱 actourism.org) This site provides information on Atlantic City's surrounding area and regional attractions, in addition to focusing on the city itself. It includes family and athletic attractions.

Each casino has its own variations on game rules.

Casino Games

The sights and sounds of the casino floor are designed to draw players in. Atlantic City's primary source of revenue is from the casinos, and it would be all but impossible to have an Atlantic City vacation without peering into at least one of the gargantuan, cavernous casinos located along the Boardwalk and in the Marina District.

Casino games are founded on "odds" and "luck" – while some games may require skill to increase your "odds" of winning, you still rely primarily on "luck" when the game is played. The better the "odds" of a player's bet, in general, the lower the payout if the player ends up winning.

Casino games are divided into two broad (and sometimes ill-defined) categories: slot machines and table games. Slot machines are usually played alone – that is, only one person is involved in the game. Table games generally require at least two people – a player and a dealer (or croupier). Table games are played on a specially-designed table, usually made of felt, which has imprinted on it the rules of the games and any required game elements. Slot machines have the payout rules written on the machine itself.

This section describes the basics of the most popular casino games, but it does not give specific gaming strategies or rules. Also, this section does not include all possible casino games; check with your casino to see if the game you want is available.

Remember: *All gambling is done at your own risk. Please be aware that you must be 21 years old to enter and remain in any New Jersey casino.*

SLOT MACHINES

In every casino, rows of slot machines seem to expand forever. Slots make up the bulk of floor space. Sounds of clanking coins and play music, sparkle of colorful lights, and bustle of people makes these little wonders the most popular casino game.

A slot machine comes in many shapes and sizes. The traditional slot machine consists of three wheels, adorned with symbols that spin when the player bets the required denomination (which can range from one penny to a hundred dollars or more). When the wheels stop spinning, the resulting symbols that the wheels have landed on determine whether the player has won that particular spin.

Slots are by far the easiest game to learn and to play. Except for a few variations, the only decision the player has to make is how much to bet with each spin. The more one bets, the larger the potential win (or loss). Today, most slot machines use "tickets" to pay winners (as opposed to real coins) which must be redeemed at a cashier. Modern slot machines sometimes use video machines in lieu of traditional spinning wheels, which allows for more unique themes, sounds, and animation.

BLACKJACK

BlackJack is the most popular casino card table game. It can be played on a video screen (similar to video poker and video slots), but it is most commonly played at a table with a dealer and one or more players. The dealer provides each player with two or more cards. Using a series of plays (such as "hit," "stand," etc.) the player tries to get the sum of his/her cards as close to 21 as possible without going over. To win a hand, the player must have a higher total than the dealer (who is also playing), but without going over 21. If a hand is a face card (face cards equal ten) and an ace (which equals either one or 11), that hand is called "blackjack" – the best possible hand, hence the name of the game.

ROULETTE

Roulette is a casino mainstay, and one of the easiest table games to learn. A small metallic ball is spun around a revolving wheel until it lands on a number. Whoever at the table has placed their bet on that number wins. Of course, there are other bets that can be made as well; players can bet on colors, on multiple numbers at the same time, or other variations. Players can also make multiple bets at once. While traditionally there is a human croupier spinning the wheel and handling the bets, modern roulette machines have made the game almost completely automatic.

CRAPS

In craps, players make bets based on their predicted outcome of a roll – or series of rolls – of a pair of dice. Players place their bets on the table based on how they think the dice will roll. Then the "shooter" – usually another player – will toss the dice onto the table. Like roulette, the locations of players' chips on the table determines what they expect the outcome of the dice roll to be.

Craps is one of the most popular casino games and a craps table can generate a noisy crowd. Even on a slow casino attendance day, people will be gathered around the craps table, cheering or shouting the night away.

Casino Games

POKER

Poker is a classic card game played both inside and outside of a casino environment. Traditionally, players (usually three or more) sit around a table and place bets based on whether they think they have a "better hand" (according to traditional poker hand rankings) than their opponents. Of course, players may bluff or use any number of tactics in attempts to get the bets as big as possible.

Poker requires a certain amount of skill. Novice players will first need to understand the poker hand rankings, and professionals will have well-kept secrets to winning. There are professional poker players and international poker tournaments that showcase the most talented players. There are many variations of poker, and some can be played at a standard casino table or even at a slot machine (in the form of video poker). The traditional "poker room" at many casinos allows for a more traditional experience, where players actually handle the cards and the dealer gets paid a percentage of the winning.

Not all casinos have a poker room for traditional poker games, but they all have some form of video poker or a table game version of poker.

BACCARAT

Like poker, baccarat is a card game which many times has an entire "baccarat room" devoted to it. However, unlike poker, baccarat is relatively simple to learn and requires less skill. In baccarat, two or more cards are dealt to a "player" and a "dealer," at the end of each game, whoever has the highest hand wins. It's as simple as that. People playing baccarat (there can be as many as 15) bet on whether they think the dealer or the player will win.

Some versions of baccarat are modified to be played as a standard table game. This version is sometimes called "mini-baccarat."

KENO

Keno is sort of like a cross between a miniature version of a state lottery and bingo. Players pick a series of numbers in the hopes that their picks will match what is drawn. Unlike a state lottery, however, keno can have many games per hour. Plus, keno has more variations and payout possibilities than traditional lotteries. The essential idea is the same.

BINGO

Bingo is popular both inside and outside of the casino. Everywhere from cruise ships to community centers can hold bingo games. Of course, within the casino, winning a game of bingo usually results in a monetary prize.

Bingo cards with random numbers are given to players under columns names B, I, N, G, and O. When a number is called ("B-1" for example), then all players in that game who have that number on their card may check it off. The first player who has a full row, column, or some other shape (as determined by the rules of that particular game) yells "BINGO!" and has won.

VARIATIONS AND OTHER GAMES

Many popular casino games have variations of popular standard games, with different (sometimes trademarked) names.

Spanish 21, Pai Gow Poker, and Texas Hold 'Em are all variations of popular casino games that are played in many casinos. Many other games exist as well, check with your casino to see what is available.

Each casino has its own rules on how to play their casino games. "House rules" generally vary in terms of player payouts, minimum and maximum bets, or even some fundamental rules of the games. Even if you are an affluent player, check with the casino before you begin to play to make sure you understand their variations.

Casino Games

Atlantic City

A Blackjack Table

Index

Index

Index

Index

About the Author

Dirk Vanderwilt is the executive editor and creator of the *Tourist Town Guides*® series, and author of several of the series' guides. He lives in New York City.

NOTES:

NOTES:

NOTES:

NOTES:

NOTES:

NOTES:

ʳ⁺tourist town guides®

Explore America's Fun Places

Books in the *Tourist Town Guides*® series are available at bookstores and online. You can also visit our web site for additional book and travel information. The address is:

http://www.touristtown.com

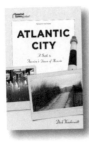

Atlantic City (4th Edition)

This guide will introduce a new facet of Atlantic City that goes beyond the appeal of its lavish casinos. Atlantic City is one of the most popular vacation destinations in the United States.

Price: $14.95; ISBN: 978-1-935455-00-4

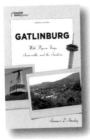

Gatlinburg (2nd Edition)

Whether it is to see the weird and wonderful displays at Ripley's Believe It or Not! Museum, or to get the adrenaline pumping with some outdoor activity or to revel in the extravaganza of Dollywood, people come to the Smokies for a variety of reasons – and they are never disappointed!

Price: $14.95; ISBN: 978-1-935455-04-2

Hilton Head

A barrier island off the coast of South Carolina, Hilton Head is a veritable coastal paradise. This destination guide gives a detailed account of this resort island, tailor made for a coastal vacation.

Price: $14.95; ISBN: 978-1-935455-06-6

Myrtle Beach (2nd Edition)

The sunsets are golden and the pace is relaxed at Myrtle Beach, the beachside playground for vacationers looking for their fill of sun, sand, and surf. Head here for the pristine beaches, the shopping opportunities, the sea of attractions, or simply to kick back and unwind.

Price: $14.95; ISBN: 978-1-935455-01-1

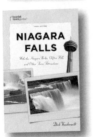

Niagara Falls (3rd Edition)

The spirited descent of the gushing falls may be the lure for you, but in Niagara Falls, it is the smorgasbord of activities and attractions that will keep you coming back for more!

Price: $14.95; ISBN: 978-1-935455-03-5

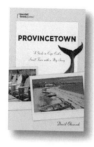

Provincetown

With a rich heritage and proud history, Provincetown is America's oldest art colony, but there is more to this place than its culture. This guide to Provincetown explores its attractions, culture, and recreation in detail to reveal a vacation destination definitely worth visiting.

Price: $13.95; ISBN: 978-1-935455-07-3

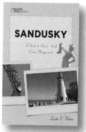

Sandusky

The Cedar Point Amusement Park may be the main reason many choose to visit Sandusky, but this comprehensive guide provides ample reason to stick around and explore the city and the neighboring islands.

Price: $13.95; ISBN: 978-0-9767064-5-8

Williamsburg

The lure to explore history is unmistakable in the town, but Williamsburg is so much more than its rich history. Head to this region to discover the modern facets of this quaint town, indulge in activities guaranteed to hook your interest, and step into the past in this historically significant destination.

Price: $14.95; ISBN: 978-1-935455-05-9

Also Available: (See http://www. touristtown.com for details)

Black Hills	Price: $14.95; ISBN: 978-0-9792043-1-9)
Breckenridge	Price: $14.95; ISBN: 978-0-9767064-9-6)
Frankenmuth	Price: $13.95; ISBN: 978-0-9767064-8-9)
Hershey	Price: $13.95; ISBN: 978-0-9792043-8-8)
Jackson Hole	Price: $14.95; ISBN: 978-0-9792043-3-3)
Key West (2nd Edition)	Price: $14.95; ISBN: 978-1-935455-02-8)
Las Vegas	Price: $14.95; ISBN: 978-0-9792043-5-7)
Mackinac	Price: $14.95; ISBN: 978-0-9767064-7-2)
Ocean City	Price: $13.95; ISBN: 978-0-9767064-6-5)
Wisconsin Dells	Price: $13.95; ISBN: 978-0-9792043-9-5)

www.touristtown.com

ORDER FORM #1
ON REVERSE SIDE

Tourist Town Guides® is published by:
Channel Lake, Inc.
P.O. Box 1771
New York, NY 10156

ORDER FORM

Telephone: With your credit card handy,
call toll-free 800.592.1566

Fax: Send this form toll-free to 866.794.5507

E-mail: Send the information on this form
to orders@channellake.com

Postal mail: Send this form with payment to Channel Lake, Inc.
P.O. Box 1771, New York, NY, 10156

Your Information: ( ) Do not add me to your mailing list

Name: _____

Address: _____

City: _____ State: _____ Zip: _____

Telephone: _____

E-mail: _____

Book Title(s) / ISBN(s) / Quantity / Price
(see previous page or www.touristtown.com for this information)

_____

_____

_____

Total payment*: $_____

Payment Information: (Circle One)   Visa / Mastercard

Number: _____ Exp: _____

Or, make check payable to: **Channel Lake, Inc.**

** Add the lesser of $6.50 USD or 18% of the total purchase price
for shipping. International orders call or e-mail first! New York
orders add 8% sales tax.*

tourist town guides®

www.touristtown.com

ORDER FORM #2
ON REVERSE SIDE

Tourist Town Guides® is published by:
Channel Lake, Inc.
P.O. Box 1771
New York, NY 10156

ORDER FORM

Telephone: With your credit card handy, call toll-free 800.592.1566

Fax: Send this form toll-free to 866.794.5507

E-mail: Send the information on this form to orders@channellake.com

Postal mail: Send this form with payment to Channel Lake, Inc. P.O. Box 1771, New York, NY, 10156

Your Information: ( ) Do not add me to your mailing list

Name: _____

Address: _____

City: _____ State: _____ Zip: _____

Telephone: _____

E-mail: _____

Book Title(s) / ISBN(s) / Quantity / Price
(see previous page or www.touristtown.com for this information)

_____

_____

_____

Total payment*: $_____

Payment Information: (Circle One) Visa / Mastercard

Number: _____ Exp: _____

Or, make check payable to: **Channel Lake, Inc.**

* Add the lesser of $6.50 USD or 18% of the total purchase price for shipping. International orders call or e-mail first! New York orders add 8% sales tax.